RAF NORTH WEALD
A PICTORIAL HISTORY

Ian,

Best wishes

Paul Peel

Dec 2010

This spread: The control tower and gate guardian at North Weald airfield, photographed in summer 2010. The Hurricane, a replica, is finished as V7313 of No 249 (Gold Coast) Squadron as flown from North Weald in the Battle of Britain in September 1940 by, among others, Pilot Officer (now Wing Commander) Tom Neil. The Hurricane was unveiled in April 2009.

Next spread: Something of a rarity—a Supermarine Spitfire Mk VI. This version of the famous fighter was the first to feature a pressurised cockpit (and a canopy which, much to the pilots' discomfiture, had to be locked shut). Only two RAF squadrons flew this mark as its principal equipment, Nos 124 and 616, and the former flew them from North Weald for a few weeks at the end of 1942 and again during the spring of the following year. The photograph, with one of North Weald's A type hangars visible in the right distance, clearly illustrates the Mk VI's extended wing tips and four-bladed propeller.

AUTHOR

RAF NORTH WEALD

A PICTORIAL HISTORY

DAVE EADE

Foreword by the Rt Hon Lord Tebbit CH

AOC PUBLICATIONS

CONTENTS

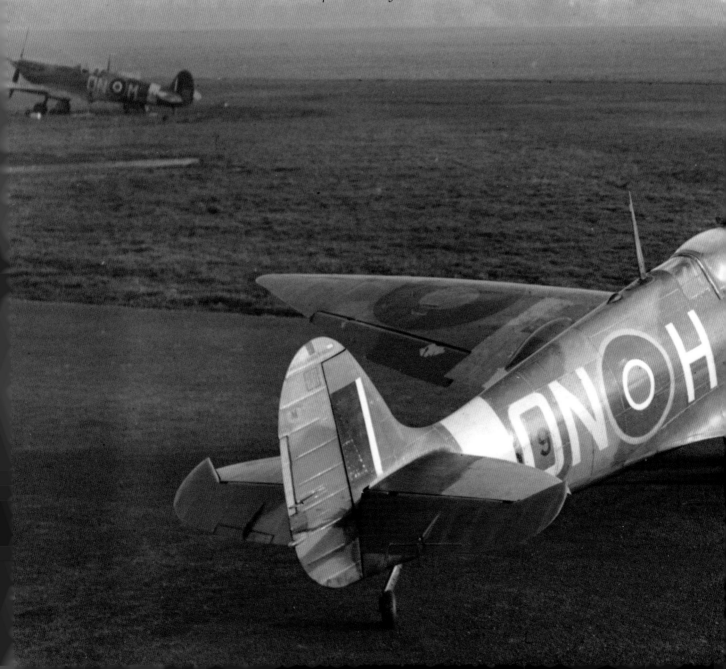

In the period since the Royal Air Force station at North Weald in Essex was closed, the United Kingdom has fought in at least four wars: the ousting of Argentine forces from their occupation of the Falkland Islands; as part of the Coalition, the removal of Iraqi forces from their illegal occupation of Kuwait and, later, the removal from power of the Saddam Hussein regime in Iraq; and, currently, combating of the Taliban insurgence in Afghanistan. At no time during that period has the United Kingdom itself been in danger of attack or invasion by the enemy in those conflicts.

The history of North Weald airfield from its birth to its close as a military establishment has always been associated with the task of protecting the United Kingdom and its capital from just such a threat. From the days of the terrifying Zeppelin airships, through the era of the might of the Nazi Luftwaffe to the early years of the threat of European domination posed by the Warsaw Pact, North Weald stood ready with its fighters to defend our skies. The cost of that mission, as with so many RAF stations, was huge in terms of lives, and a work such as this must, firstly, be dedicated to those men and women who were lost.

I should like to record my thanks to those whose work, both illustrative and written, is included in the book and to those whose help was invaluable in producing it. Four people deserve special mention. I am most grateful to the Rt Hon. Lord Tebbit CH, who very kindly consented to provide the Foreword. Next, without the help of Arthur Moreton, the North Weald Airfield Historian *in situ*, the record you see would never have been completed: his vast knowledge of the Station is second to none, and his enthusiasm for this volume has been unstinting. I should also like to mention Air Commodore Roger Topp AFC**, whose association with North Weald in the days of the 'Black Arrows' aerobatic team and his continuing involvement with the airfield—and his very welcome support for my earlier book about RAF Wattisham—led to a conversation at an Ad Hoc reception in the summer of 2009 that sowed the seed. His qualities of leadership continue to this day! Finally credit must go to the man who is Ad Hoc Publications—Roger Chesneau. His signature, as with all his work, is all over this book, and his guidance and encouragement have been invaluable.

Many other individuals and organisations have generously lent their support for the project: Roger Cook, Mick Davis (Cross & Cockade International), Tom Docherty (No 72 Squadron Association), James Ivers (No 601 Squadron Association), Kennet Aviation, Henry Milne, the North Weald Airfield Museum (NWAM), Phil Jarrett, Graham Jessop, Johan Junemo, Roger Lindsay, John Meddows, Geoff Monahan, Jim Molder, Tom Moulson, Ted Reeve, Denis Shrosbree, The Squadron, Pip Stowell (No 151 Squadron Association), Peter Teichman, Michael Thurley, Dick Ward and Weald Aviation Services Ltd. I thank them all.

Dave Eade
Stowmarket, October 2010

ROYAL AIR FORCE NORTH WEALD STATION OFFICERS COMMANDING

SQUADRON COMMANDERS[1]
Maj. A. H. Morton, No 39 (HD) Sqn (00/07/16)
Maj. C. A. Ridley, No 75 Sqn (00/05/18)
Maj. C.O. Brand, No 75 Sqn (00/06/19)
Maj. A. T. Harris, No 44 Sqn (00/07/19)[2]
Station closed 00/12/19

STATION COMMANDERS
Wg Cdr A. G. R. Garrod MC DFC (27/09/27)
Wg Cdr W. S. Douglas MC DFC (06/01/28)
Wg Cdr B. E. Smythes DFC (16/08/29)
Wg Cdr R. G. D. Small (01/08/30)
Wg Cdr R. H. G . Neville OBE MC (17/12/32)
Wg Cdr G. B. A. Baker MC (14/12/33)
Wg Cdr T. Q. Studd DFC (13/12/34)
Wg Cdr J. N. Dand MBE (06/08/37)
Gp Capt. D. F. Lucking (10/07/39)
Gp Capt. H. B. Frew DSO MC AFC (07/09/39)
Wg Cdr H. D. O'Neill (31/12/39)
Wg Cdr F. V. Beamish DSO DFC AFC (07/06/40)
Gp Capt. S. F. Vincent DFC AFC (20/03/41)
Gp Capt. T . G. Pike DFC (02/02/42)
Gp Capt. D. G. Morris (05/08/42)

Gp Capt. M. W. S. Robinson CBE (13/09/43)
Wg Cdr P. G. Wykeham-Barnes DSO DFC (07/02/44)
Wg Cdr C. A. Pritchard DFC (09/03/44)
Gp Capt. G. L. Denholm DFC (03/10/44)
Wg Cdr R. Barton DFC (09/02/45)
Wg Cdr H. L. Hallowes DFC DFM (13/03/45)
Wg Cdr W. R. Hartwright (11/06/45)
Wg Cdr W. R. Beman OBE (29/09/45)
Gp Capt. D. R. S. Bader DSO* DFC* (00/09/45–00/03/46?)[3]

Wg Cdr J. H. Page OBE (18/03/47)
Wg Cdr R. Bain GD (25/10/48)
Wg Cdr J. D. Ronald AFC (19/12/49)
Wg Cdr P. G. Wykeham-Barnes DSO DFC (30/12/51)
Wg Cdr A. C. Deere OBE DSO DFC (30/05/52)
Gp Capt. G. C. Eversleigh OBE AFC (00/06/54)
Gp Capt. R. J. Gosnell DSO DFC (15/10/55)
Gp Capt. J Rankine DSO DFC (01/03/56)
Wg Cdr F. B. Sutton (08/01/57)
Sqn Ldr G. Gray (15/08/58)[4]
Flt Lt D. R. W. Hammersbek (05/11/58)
Flt Lt M. J. Monaghan (14/09/60)
Sqn Ldr F. W. Alder (24/09/62)

Sqn Ldr D. A. Austin (10/02/64)
Station closed 28/08/64

Notes
1. Airfield opened as Royal Flying Corps landing ground commanded by Squadron Commanders.
2. Later to become Sir Arthur 'Bomber' Harris.
3. Contrary to popular belief, the famous 'legless' fighter ace Douglas Bader was never stationed at North Weald while World War II was being fought in Europe. Following his release from captivity in the infamous Colditz Castle, he was posted to North Weald as RAF Fighter Commander, North Weald Sector, on 24 July 1945, with ten fighter squadrons and six operational airfields under his command. While at North Weald Bader made 191 flights and led the 300 aircraft that took part in the first Battle of Britain Fly Past over London on 15 September 1945. He served at the airfield until his retirement from the RAF in March 1946.
4. Sqn Ldr 'Jed' Gray placed RAF North Weald over from an operational station to Care and Maintenance on 15 November 1958.

FOREWORD

The Rt Hon. Lord Tebbit CH

Above: Pilot Officer Norman Tebbit, photographed in the early 1950s while serving at RAF North Weald. Lord Tebbit is the President of the North Weald Airfield Museum.

COURTESY NWAM

AS I pass North Weald on my journeys to and from London my eyes are always drawn to the hangars, and most of all to those alongside the M11 motorway. It was this part of the airfield that was home to No 604, The County of Middlesex Squadron, Royal Auxiliary Air Force, and I cannot stop my mind going back to my days on the Squadron, flying Vampires and Meteors almost sixty years ago.

Old airfields do not have the romantic visual appeal of mediæval castles, but to those that know them there is something no less redolent of the past in the old runways, hangars, flight lines and control towers than in turreted towers and moats. There is something still there of the men and women, and of the machines, whose lives, and often deaths, were rooted in those structures which still remain all these years on.

Born out of the need to defend London from air attack by Zeppelins, the story of North Weald embraces the history of the growth of air power from early beginnings to the height of the Cold War, and now how the amazing collections of privately owned military and civil aircraft have made it their home.

Dave Eade's history of North Weald records its birth in the spring of 1916 and its rôle guarding London against both Zeppelins and the great Gotha bombers of the First World War before, in another era of defence cut-backs, it was left in Care and Maintenance from 1919 until, in 1926, the far-sighted Hugh Trenchard authorised a return to front-line status as home to Nos 56 and 29 Squadrons.

With the outbreak of the Second World War, North Weald truly came into its own again, receiving not only RAF squadrons but the American Eagle Squadrons; the Norwegians, whose special relationship with the place is marked by the memorial at the Station's main gate; and then the Czechoslovakians and the Poles, who continued their countries' struggles for freedom from this corner of Essex.

As the Iron Curtain came down across Europe, North Weald readied itself for war once again and welcomed, first, No 601 (County of London) and then No 604 (County of Middlesex) Squadrons, and soon after that No 72 Squadron too.

By the time I joined No 604 in early 1952 the Squadron was equipped with the Vampire 3, which I had not previously flown, but later that year we moved up to the Meteor 8, which I flew until the pressures of civil flying and marriage became too much and I stood down after three wonderful years, losing contact with North Weald until being elected as the Member of Parliament for Epping in 1970.

In this story of RAF North Weald there is so much of the best of the history of flying and of Britain through the twentieth century. It has about it the tang of aviation fuel, the comradeship of aviation, The King's Head in North Weald, The Thatched House and The George and Dragon in Epping, and the cemetery at St Andrew's Church.

It is a good story, very well told.

Norman Tebbit

PRELUDE

WHEN, on Thursday 17 December 1903, Wilbur and Orville Wright made the first manned, powered aeroplane flight in the United States, it stimulated great interest in aviation throughout the world—including, of course, Europe. For the previous two hundred years, man had striven with balloons, kites and gliders to master the skies, but success in building a flyable heavier-than-air machine eluded him for many years. That first flight lasted some twelve seconds and covered a distance of about 120 feet. What is not often recorded is the fact that on the same day the Wrights made three further flights, achieving a maximum distance of 852 feet in 59 seconds. Over the ensuing years, the Wrights' aeroplane, the Flyer, was demonstrated to the public in North America and Europe and also, more importantly, to the US War Department, which placed an order for three Flyer III machines.

Throughout the United States and Europe, engineers strove to emulate and surpass the Wright Brothers' achievement. By 1909, names that were later to become synonymous with aviation were struggling to produce practical designs that would take man to the skies. In Great Britain, Samuel Cody and Claude Grahame-White were building machines, while A. V. Roe, whose company Avro would go on to build such iconic aircraft as the Lancaster and Vulcan, was constructing aeroplanes at his workshops in Walthamstow and at Brooklands. The most famous of all his early designs was the Avro 504, which remained in service for many years as the military trainer of choice. In Europe, Voisin, Fokker and Louis Blériot were building early monoplanes—and Blériot was to become famous for completing the first successful manned airborne crossing of the English Channel, a feat accomplished on 25 July 1909.

Particular encouragement for the development of aviation in Britain was forthcoming from two newspaper proprietors, Alfred and Harold Harmsworth, later to become Lords Northcliffe and Rothermere, respectively. These two gentlemen owned the *Daily Mail*. Under the banner of their newspaper they proffered prizes for races and achievement, and in

BALLOONLESS AIRSHIP.

(From Our Own Correspondent.)

NEW YORK, Friday, Dec. 18.

Messrs. Wilbur and Orville Wright, of Ohio, yesterday successfully experimented with a flying machine at Kittyhawk, North Carolina. The machine had no balloon attachment, and derives its force from propellers worked by a small engine.

In the face of a wind blowing twenty-one miles an hour the machine flew three miles at the rate of eight miles an hour, and descended at a point selected in advance. The idea of the box-kite was used in the construction of the airship.

Above: A newspaper cutting of the remarkable events of 17 December 1903 by a reporter who has apparently failed to grasp their significance—and has got some details wrong!

Below: What is generally accepted as being the first manned, sustained and controlled flight in a heavier-than-air machine took place at Kitty Hawk, North Carolina on 17 December 1903, with Orville Wright at the controls of the Flyer and his brother Wilbur in attendance alongside. This photograph was taken to record the event. Notice the launching rail stretching across the left foreground.

Right: During the first decade of the twentieth century, aviation pioneers were busy refining their creations not only in North America but in Europe too. The Frenchman Louis Blériot was one of the most successful: it was he who made the first airborne crossing of the English Channel, on 25 July 1909, in the process winning the £1,000 prize offered by the *Daily Mail* for the achievement. Below: Amongst the pioneers working in Great Britain was Claude Grahame-White, who was based at Hendon in north London. Part of his original factory has been incorporated into the RAF Museum.

Right: The county of Essex has very strong links with early aviation in Britain, not least through Alliott Verdon Roe, who for a period in the spring of 1909 operated from workshops located beneath a pair of railway arches crossing the Waltham-stow Marshes, where he is seen making adjustments to his triplane in this photograph.

1912 they sponsored the first air race around London. Public interest in this 'Aerial Derby' was such that crowds gathered along the route to follow the competitors, gaping in wonder at the flimsy machines. In September that year one Lieutenant Gray of the Royal Flying Corps landed his aircraft at Chipping Ongar, some five miles from North Weald Bassett, but the first recorded flying incident in North Weald proper was in 1913, when a Deperdussin flown by one Lieutenant Porte crash-landed at Curr's Farm while taking part in the second round-London air race.

Improvement in design and performance also stemmed from another, rather different aspect of aviation—the skills and daring of the 'barn-stormers'. Providing thrills (and spills) to the general public, these pilots took their lives in their hands to carry out stunts at fêtes and fairs all over the world. Enthusiasts of today owe a debt of gratitude to these aerial

9

AD HOC COLLECTION

Left: The first recorded incident of an aeroplane landing in the vicinity of North Weald occurred in the morning on 6 September 1912, when Lieutenant Spenser Gray, of the Royal Flying Corps' Naval Wing, landed his Deperdussin Monoplane, serial number 7, near the Red Cow public house in Chipping Ongar. Following one abortive take-off in which the aeroplane was slightly damaged, the pilot, who was *en route* from Eastchurch to Hardwicke and taking part in Army manœuvres, effected repairs and departed the following morning.

exponents as the latter's antics led to what is always regarded as the first true air show, that held at Reims in France in August 1909. The excitement generated by this event paved the way for many more such gatherings all over the Continent, while on 10 May 1910 Claude Grahame-White successfully staged the first British show at Hendon, on the northern outskirts of London.

In 1914, however, sinister events were to put a stop to all the aerial entertainment, as military strategists and tacticians and aeroplane manufacturers turned their attention to how this new phenomenon in the sky could best be turned to their advantage in the conflict that threatened to engulf Europe.

At that time, despite the fact that effective and reliable flying machines were in their infancy—only five years or so had elapsed since the first sustained flight over British soil—the possibilities of their being used for aerial bombardment and other offensive purposes were exercising

1907 Training

From The Essex Imperial Yeomanry Magazine, *February 1907*

'The Annual training of the Regiment will take place at Weald Hall, North Weald, near Epping. Date of assembly, Friday, May 24th, date of dismissal, Saturday, June 8th. A pleasant site has been selected for the camp in a field belonging to Mr. S. Powell, of Weald Hall.

'Horses will be picketted in the lines, it being Lord Methuen's wish that stabling should be dispensed with. The experience of other regiments who have discarded stabling for picketting is unanimously in favour of the latter method, and apart from any other advantages, there will be great saving in expense to the regiment. Weald Hall is one mile from North Weald station and telegraph, and two miles from Epping.'

COURTESY NWAM

Above: A passenger train of the Great Eastern Railway chugging along the Epping–Ongar branch line. The railway here, which passed through North Weald, influenced the choice of the village as a military centre.

"Has anyone ever thought of the great possibility Epping offers for a flying centre? Take the case of the large tract of level ground just outside the town, opposite the Isolation Hospital at North Weald, from the Turnpike Cottage northwards, for nearly a mile on the left of the road.

"The existence of this land should be made well known . . . and a splendid aerodrome could result—only 17 miles away from the Metropolis!

"If such a place were constructed it would mean prosperity to our town in many ways. Firstly Epping would become famous; secondly builders and tradesmen would profit by the buildings to be erected for, and the provisions to be supplied to, the airmen, mechanics and officials who would reside there . . ."

Above: One resident of Epping, the market town a couple of miles from North Weald, was evidently impressed by having witnessed the novel spectacle of aeroplanes flying and made this suggestion in a local newspaper in 1911. His wishes were to be fulfilled.

Right: A simplified map showing North Weald Bassett and its environs in 1900. In earlier centuries, the village was usually referred to as 'Weald Gullet', after the small stream that ran though its centre.

military minds. It seemed unlikely that winged aircraft would for some years be able to lift anything effective in terms of a payload—it was as much as they could do to carry the engine aloft—but dirigible airships were another matter: in Germany in particular, they had demonstrated a capability for carrying large numbers of passengers, and across huge distances, in safety—and if passengers, why not something unpleasant instead? By the end of the 1914, as predicted, airships had begun to appear over Britain from across the waters, releasing bombs. These very early raids were, in truth, derisory pinpricks, but they were the harbinger of nastier things to come.

Meanwhile, in the open fields dotted around the hamlet of North Weald Bassett in Essex, all was relatively quiet. The villagers had been used to a military presence in the neighbourhood. There had been a fort at Weald Gullet, with a theoretical establishment of half a dozen guns, while, to the north-west, an area of land adjacent to Weald Hall had been utilised a camp for the Essex Imperial Yeomanry. North Weald was handily located from the Army's point of view. It was less than twenty miles from London, and close to the main London—Norwich road. There was a post office and a telegraph office (though not yet a telephone connection), and there was piped water. Most importantly, the Great Eastern Railway ran alongside the village, with a station and goods yard at Weald Gullet, not far from the old Army post.

With the threatening presence of Zeppelins beginning to make itself felt in 1915, the War Office was goaded into taking steps to protect London, and by the end of the year pilots of No 39 (Home Defence) Squadron of the Royal Flying Corps were operating out of two aerodromes in west Essex, at Suttons Farm (later to become RAF Hornchurch) and at Hainault Farm near Ilford. Within a few months it had been decided to establish a third 'landing ground', and those peaceful green fields to the north of Weald Gullet would soon resound to the noise of aero engines . . .

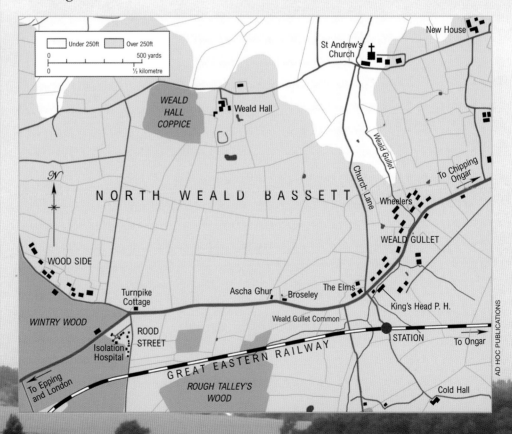

TERROR FROM THE SKIES

WITH the coming of war in 1914, attention was focused on the mainland of Europe—only to be sharply redirected in January 1915 with the arrival in British skies of the first giant airship. Known generically as 'Zeppelins'—though in fact originating both from that company and from the Schütte Lanz organisation—these intimidating craft brought an entirely new dimension to the conflict.

Quite apart from the death and destruction that it threatened to unleash, the sight of one of these monsters alone must have been terrifying, if only for its sheer size. The early airships were nearly 550 feet long and had a diameter of some 61 feet. They held over 1.1 million cubic feet of gas and were powered by four very noisy Maybach engines. Later models reached a length of over 644 feet and 78 feet in diameter. They had a range of some 1,300 miles (which for its day was very impressive), they could reach heights in excess of 12,000 feet and they travelled at speeds of up to 55 miles per hour. Typically, a crew of nineteen was on board. Not only, given their huge size and the noise they made, were these raiders extremely frightening, their destructive warload—limited at first but soon massively increased to perhaps four 300kg and forty 60kg bombs, plus up to sixty incendiaries each weighing 10kg—was sufficient to gain the respect of both military and civilian observers on the ground. It was a totally new form of warfare, and the civilian population, having never before been subjected to these aerial bombardments, was being terrorised.

Several raids over the eastern counties of England are recorded, the targets principally dock areas and military production sites along the East

Above: The aerial bombardment of the civilian population was an entirely new phenomenon, and one to which a viable response was lacking. There was plenty of official advice, however, as exemplified by this leaflet.

Above: German World War I bombs. The 60kg projectile is to the left and the 300kg at centre; at right is a 1,000kg bomb, which armed German R-Planes towards the end of the war.
Left: A map showing the principal German Zeppelin bases and the location of the British Home Defence squadrons, June 1916.

AD HOC COLLECTION

Above: Home Defence aircraft were fitted with a variety of weapons—some quickly perceived to be impractical—for attacking Zeppelins, but the principal objective was to ignite the airship's hydrogen-filled envelope. B.E.2cs were thus commonly equipped with a single, movable Lewis gun that could fire both standard and incendiary ammunition.
Below: A No 39 Squadron B.E.2c, showing the type's semi-exposed V8 engine and right-angled exhaust stacks.

Coast and the Thames Estuary. Attacks on the city of London were forbidden by the German High Command in the early days of the war, but in May 1915 this ruling was rescinded and raids on the capital became commonplace.

The appearance of airships over London caused unrest amongst the public: the enemy appeared to be attacking the civilian population with impunity. Under this pressure, the Government was forced to initiate defensive measures, and as a result the Home Defence Force, consisting of ten squadrons (later reduced to eight) was created within the Royal Flying Corps with the express purpose of defending vulnerable localities. Air intelligence associated with the Zeppelin raids was supported by the interception of radio transmissions, received before the airships took off and throughout their passage.

Within a year, an airfield at North Weald Bassett had been prepared, and it was declared operational in spring 1916, accommodating 'A' flight of No 39 Squadron—a unit formed out of No 19 Reserve Aeroplane Squadron, which was already operating from two nearby aerodromes, Hainault Farm and Suttons Farm. Its primary task was the defence of the capital, and for this purpose it was equipped with B.E.2c fighters. Although proven to be unsuitable as a day fighter on the Front in Europe and no match for the Luftwaffe's *Dreidecker* (triplane) aircraft, the B.E.2c was ideal as a night fighter, offering a steady gun platform in the battle against the Zeppelins. Normally consisting of five aircraft, 'A' Flight was commanded by Captain L. S. Ross.

COURTESY CROSS & COCKADE INTERNATIONAL

THE AIR DEFENCE OF BRITAIN: ORDER OF BATTLE, JUNE 1916

Unit	Bases	No of aircraft on strength
No 28 Squadron	Gosport	2 × B.E.12
	Newhaven	—
No 33 Squadron	Bramham Moor	4 × B.E.2c
	Beverley	1 × B.E.12
	Coal Aston	—
	Doncaster	1 × B.E.12
No 36 Squadron	Cramlington	3 × B.E.12, 6 × B.E.2c, 2 × Bristol Scout
	Seaton Carew	—
	Turnhouse	—
No 39 Squadron	Hounslow	3 × B.E.12, 6 B.E.2c, 2 × Bristol Scout
	Hainault Farm	2 × B.E.12, 4 B.E.2c, 1 × Bristol Scout
	North Weald Bassett	To receive aircraft from Hounslow August 1915
	Suttons Farm	1 × B.E.12, 4 B.E.2c, 1 × Bristol Scout
No 50 Squadron	Dover	3 × B.E.12, 2 × B.E.2c
	Wye	—
No 51 Squadron	Thetford	—
	Narborough	—
	Norwich	3 × B.E.2c
No 52 Squadron	Hounslow	2 × B.E.12, 3 × B.E.2c
	Goldhanger	—
	Rochford	—
No 54 Squadron	Castle Bromwich	4 × B.E.2c
	Lilbourne	—
	Papplewick	—
	Waddington	—

ROYAL AIRCRAFT FACTORY B.E.2c
Type: Light reconnaissance, fighting and bombing biplane
Engines: One 70hp Renault V8 or 90hp R.A.F. 1a V8
Length: 27ft 3in (8.31m)
Wing span: 37ft 0in (11.28m)
Speed: 86mph (138kph) maximum
Endurance: 3¼hrs
Armament: One movable 0.303in Lewis gun and up to 220lb (100kg) bomb load
Crew: Two (pilot and gunner)

Left: The organisation of Home Defence aeroplanes in response to the Zeppelin threat, June 1916 (see also map on page 12). In most instances the theoretical establishment for each Flight was well in excess of the numbers given.
Below: A formal portrait of Second Lieutenant Wulstan Tempest RFC.

Early flights and 'scrambles' were found to be very frustrating, but on the night of 3 September 1916 Lieutenant William Leefe Robinson, flying from Suttons Farm—later to become RAF Hornchurch—in B.E.2c 2693 succeeded in bringing down the airship SL 11; and one month later a pilot based at North Weald Bassett had similar success. Fying B.E.2c 4577, Second Lieutenant Wulstan Joseph Tempest had taken off from North Weald on 1 October 1916 and found himself at some 14,000 feet over the eastern outskirts of London just before midnight. At the same time the German airship L 31 was caught in a tripod of searchlight beams. Tempest saw the illuminated L 31 and headed towards it at full throttle.

A faulty fuel pump gave him handling difficulties in the chase, and he had to pump the fuel with one hand while flying his aeroplane with the

Left: Equipping Home Defence squadrons to meet the Zeppelin threat tended to be a haphazard business. There was no 'standard', proven aeroplane and availability was an important factor in terms of procurement. Hence No 39 Squadron flew several different types. While the B.E.2c was, at first, the most numerous, its development the B.E.2e was also used, and this example is was photographed outside the aeroplane sheds at North Weald. The sheds could be closed by means of canvas curtains, as seen here.

COURTESY NWAM

Above: The B.E.2e differed from the earlier B.E.2c in having unequal-span wings, a more powerful engine and greater range. This example, 7216, is fitted with rails for firing Le Prieur anti-Zeppelin rockets. Home Defence pilots considered these French-designed projectiles to be of limited value and indeed no airships appear ever to have been attacked by aeroplanes firing them.

other; moreover, with the skies full of shells from the anti-aircraft guns below, flying in close proximity to an illuminated airship was not the safest place to be. Tempest eventually manœuvred himself to a position to the rear of the mighty L 31, and, changing hands from yoke to pump and then to gun, he fired a massive volley into the underside of the Zeppelin before turning again under the rear fins to repeat the exercise. In his report afterwards, Tempest likened the result of his attack to a giant Chinese lantern in the sky, which slowly turned pink and then red as the huge gas cells ignited.

Still in grave danger, with the flaming airship now falling from the sky above his aircraft, Tempest put his aeroplane into a spinning dive in order to escape the fireball and headed back for North Weald Bassett. His drama was not over yet, though, because his violent escape manœuvres had brought about an attack of vertigo and air-sickness that threatened to overwhelm him. His arrival and final approach in the early hours of the morning of the 2nd, to the now fogbound airfield, was too fast and his

Right: A profile of a B.E.2c, with conjectural detail depicting 4577, the aeroplane that Tempest was flying on the night of 1/2 October 1916. The entire crew of L 31 perished when the airship was shot down in flames, including its prominent and influential commander, Kapitänleutnant Heinrich Mathy.

4577

An Awesome Sight

Eyewitness accounts of the demise of L 31

'Tempest was dining out with friends [and his fiancée] at a doctor's house in Epping High Street [commented Mr Sidney Hills of Epping] when the alarm came. The story is told that before taking off the airman arranged to fire five Very lights if he was successful in shooting down the Zeppelin. The intrepid Tempest kept his word.

'Firing incendiary bullets into airships from underneath, he set it on fire. Spellbound onlookers from near and far witnessed an awesome sight they never forgot. A bright light, like a star, shone out from the airship, held in many searchlights. Bigger and bigger grew the light, until at last the whole Zeppelin was a blazing inferno. Breaking into several parts, it crashed to earth in Potters Bar.

'The cheering of jubilant crowds could be heard from miles away. We watched the sight from our flat on the second floor of an Epping High Street Garage; and afterwards with many more went out to the High Street to welcome back Lieutenant Tempest, as he rode in on his motorcycle combination, cheered by Epping folk. It was said that he wholly finished his interrupted dinner—a meal well earned.

The Zeppelin looked 'no larger than a cucumber,' remarked Mr A. J. Hyde of Coopersale. 'Suddenly what appeared to be a Very light was seen. Immediately the guns stopped firing and the searchlights switched off. For several minutes nothing seemed to happen, then what looked like an orange glow appeared. Then suddenly we saw flames, small at first, then becoming like a gigantic bonfire. By this time we could see the whole of the Zeppelin being burned . . . it broke into two pieces and the impression one got was of two large flaming parrot cages. . . . Many people were heard cheering but I remember several people saying, "Poor devils, they're being roasted alive—but that's war."'

One Crew Captured and Two Consumed by Fire

COURTESY NWAM

COMBAT REPORT BY SECOND LIEUTENANT WULSTAN TEMPEST, 2 OCTOBER 1916
'Sir—I have the honour to report that on 1st October at 10 p.m. I left the ground on [sic] B.E.2c 4577 to patrol between Joyce Green and Hainault. Approximately at 11.40 I first sighted a Zeppelin. I immediately made for her and fired one drum which took effect at once and set her on fire at about 12,700 ft. I then proceeded to North Weald to land and wrecked the machine on the aerodrome, without hurting myself, at 12.10 a.m.'

Below: A No 39 (HD) Squadron pilot poses with his B.E.2e at North Weald. Notice the external fuel tank fitted beneath the upper mainplane.

landing removed the main undercarriage. He was quickly extracted from the wreck, suffering only a mild cut and a headache. The mighty L 31 was totally destroyed in its subsequent crash at Potters Bar some thirteen miles to the north-west of North Weald, many of the crew preferring the leap from the falling craft to the flame-consuming alternative.

On 13 October Tempest was awarded the Distinguished Service Order for his exploits that night, and the event has been commemorated with the naming of Tempest Avenue in Potters Bar and Tempest Mead in North Weald.

In May 1917 the Germans, having carried out 51 Zeppelin raids over the British Isles—killing 557 people and injuring 1,358 in the process— began using a new weapon for their attacks. This came in the form of the

Left: Little evidence of No 39 Squadron's time at North Weald survives, but this HD pattern aeroplane shed is still (2010) *in situ* at Moreton, a village some four miles to the north-east— and it has been established that it is indeed one of the sheds from North Weald aerodrome. There are plans to move the structure so that it may be preserved.

AUTHOR

ROYAL AIRCRAFT FACTORY
B.E.12a
Type: Light reconnaissance, fighting and bombing biplane
Engines: One 140hp R.A.F. 4a V12
Length: 27ft 3in (8.31m)
Wing span: 40ft 6in (13.29m)
Speed: 105mph (169kph) maximum
Endurance: 3hrs
Armament: One movable 0.303in Vickers gun and (optionally) two 112lb (51kg) bombs
Crew: Pilot only

Right, upper: The B.E.12a was also introduced to service with No 39 Squadron at North Weald, the first recorded sortie from the aerodrome being in March 1917.

Right, lower: At least one Armstrong-Whitworth F.K.8 was issued to No 39 Squadron, and this aircraft, B237, is recorded as having carried out an early-morning patrol from North Weald on 22 July 1917. The style of markings depicted here is conjectural.

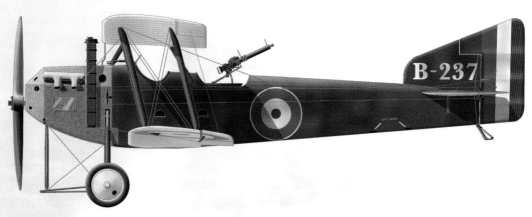

Above: The cockpit of a replica B.E.2c, showing the very rudimentary controls and flight instruments.

Right: A map showing the general layout of North Weald aerodrome in late 1916. The site occupied 136 acres, with approximate dimensions of 900 by 850 yards This early period of its use as a military airfield was officially terminated on 20 February 1920.

huge Gotha and Giant bombers. Armed with three 0.312-inch machine guns, each aircraft was capable of carrying about a ton of bombs (although in practice individual payloads rarely exceeded 1,000 pounds) over a range in excess of 500 miles and at a top speed of some 87mph. With a height capability of over 21,000 feet, the aircraft were all but

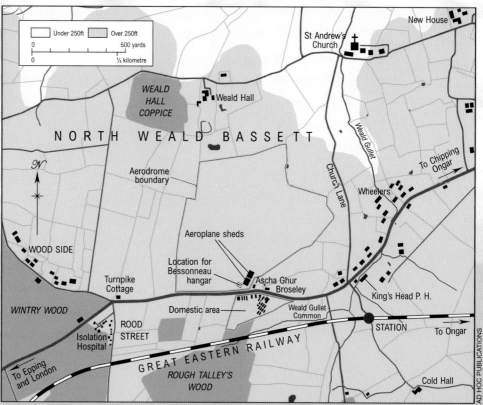

BRISTOL F.2B
Type: Fighter-reconnaissance biplane
Engines: One 190hp Rolls-Royce Falcon I, 220hp Falcon II or 275hp Falcon III
Length: 25ft 10in (7.87m)
Wing span: 39ft 3in (11.96m)
Speed: 113mph (182kph) maximum (Falcon III)
Endurance: 3hrs
Armament: One fixed 0.303in Vickers gun and one or two movable 0.303in Lewis guns, plus up to twelve 25lb (11kg) bombs
Crew: Pilot and gunner

Left, upper: What would today be considered primitive flying capabilities led to many aircraft coming to grief, especially in landing accidents. No 39 Squadron's B.E.12 6495 experienced such a 'prang' at North Weald.
Left, lower: Lieutenant A. J. Arkell and Air Mechanic A. T. C. Stagg, with canine companion, pose with F.2B C4636 following their victory over a Gotha bomber.

invulnerable to the fighters of the day. Both bomber types showed great resilience during the conflict, but during the night of 19/20 May 1918 Lieutenant A. J. Arkell of No 39 (HD) Squadron and his gunner Air Mechanic A. T. C. Stagg, flying Bristol F.2B C4636 from North Weald, managed to shoot down a Gotha bomber over East Ham.

The Bristol Fighter had, in its original F.2A form, begun to reach Royal Flying Corps units at the end of 1916 and its improved successor the F.2B

Left: A Bristol F.2B of No 39 (HD) Squadron. The aeroplane, B1390, is a presentation 'Brisfit' and the prominent inscription reads 'Presented by Maharaja Bahadur Sir Rameshwar Singh of Darbangha No. 5'. A considerable number of the RFC/RAF's aircraft were marked in this way, indicating that they had been funded using money specially donated by individuals and organisations, frequently from overseas. The practice was again widespread in World War II.

Above: A Gotha G.V twin-engined bomber of the type used in raids over the British Isles from 1917.

AD HOC COLLECTION

HD Pattern aeroplane sheds
(two coupled units)

Workshops

Technical store

Dope store

Blacksmith's shop

Apron

Aeroplane store

Butts

Telephone room

Site for Bessonneau hangar

Royal Engineers' store

Guard house

ASCHA GHUR

BROSELEY

Machine gun store

Later entrance

Bomb store

Main entrance

PUBLIC HIGHWAY

Domestic site

AD HOC PUBLICATIONS

Above, right: The layout of the principal airfield buildings at North Weald in 1917–18. There appears to be no firm evidence that the canvas Bessonneau hangar was ever erected. The aerodrome proper was, of course, exclusively grassed.

was operational by the spring of 1917; its first recorded offensive sorties in the hands of No 39 Squadron pilots took place during the early morning of 6 December that year when Second Lieutenant C. P. Donnison (with Lieutenant W. N. Fraser) and Lieutenant C. J. Chabot (with Lieutenant V. A. Lanos) took A7249 and C4823, respectively, aloft from North Weald in response to a German bombing raid on London. The 'Brisfit', as it was affectionately known, represented a considerable improvement over the relatively slow and vulnerable B.E.s and had the inestimable advantage

Right: Profile showing the Bristol F.2B in which nineteen-year-old Lieutenant Tony Arkell and Air Mechanic Albert Stagg intercepted and shot down a Gotha on the night of 19/20 May 1918. The aircraft bore the nickname 'Devil in the Dusk'. Some of the details depicted in this artwork are speculative.
Below: B1390 and other Bristol F.2Bs, photographed at North Weald Bassett in 1918.

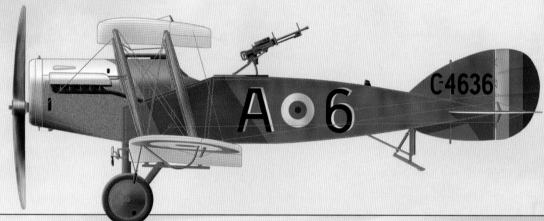

A ● 6   C-4636

COURTESY PHILIP JARRETT

Left: A Sopwith Camel of No 44 Squadron roars over its home field—probably Hainault Farm, just prior to its move to North Weald. Notice the 'Zeppelin' type wind vane and the curtaining on the aeroplane shed. The night fighter version of the Camel—often referred to as the Sopwith 'Comic'—had its armament removed from the cowling and fitted on the upper wing, and the pilot's upward visibility was much improved by the fashioning of additional 'cutouts', just visible here, in the wing itself.

over the latter of featuring a fixed, forward-firing machine gun in addition to the flexibly mounted weapon amidships. Indeed, such was the versatility of the F.2B that it remained in service in various rôles for well over a decade.

On 1 April 1918 the Royal Flying Corps was absorbed into the newly established Royal Air Force. On 22 May elements of a second Home Defence squadron, No 75, arrived at North Weald, headquartered at Goldington in Bedfordshire and with flights based at the Suffolk aerodromes at Hadleigh and Elmswell and elsewhere. Its principal equipment was the trusty Avro 504K, but it also operated a few B.E.12s. The rotary-engine Avro was essentially a training aeroplane, but a large number had been adapted for the night-fighting rôle by having the front cockpit faired over and a mounting for a .303 Lewis machine gun added, the weapon firing over the upper wing. Spare ammunition drums for reloading were carried in a rack adjacent to the pilot.

At the beginning of November 1918, No 39 Squadron moved from North Weald to France but saw little or no action since within days, on the 11th of the month, the Armistice was signed, bringing an end to the war in Europe. The predictable postwar economies were swiftly implemented, and No 75 Squadron was disbanded in June 1919. This did not quite mark the end of this first phase of activities at North Weald, however, because

SOPWITH 1F.1 CAMEL
Type: Fighter
Engine: One 110hp Le Rhône 9J rotary
Length: 18ft 8in (5.69m)
Wing span: 28ft 0in (8.53m)
Speed: 111mph (179kph) max.
Endurance: 2–2½hrs
Armament: Two 0.303in Vickers guns on forward fuselage or (night fighter) two 0.303in Lewis guns on upper wing
Crew: Pilot only

Below: A night-fighter conversion of an Avro 504K, the RFC's widely used training aircraft. A single Lewis gun was mounted on the upper plane, and in most aircraft (though not in this example) the front cockpit was faired over, while some also had simplified main undercarriages.

Above: A rather hazy close-up of the Lewis gun mounting on an Avro 504K night fighter.
Right: An Avro 504K night fighter with a modified under-carriage awaits its next sortie.

AVRO 504K NIGHT FIGHTER
Type: Converted trainer
Engine: One 110hp Le Rhône rotary
Length: 29ft 5in (8.97m)
Wing span: 36ft 0in (10.97m)
Weight: 1,830lb (830kg) loaded
Speed: 95mph (153kph) max.
Range: 250 miles (400km)
Endurance: 3hrs
Armament: One 0.303in Lewis gun on upper wing
Crew: Pilot only

Right: Profile of a standard Sopwith 1F.1 Camel serving with No 44 Squadron.
Below: The modified twin Lewis gun armament of a Camel night fighter. As can be seen, the weapons could be pulled down via curved racks to enable the pilot to change the ammunition drums when required.

on 1 July No 44 Squadron, equipped with the renowned Sopwith Camel (many of the aeroplanes adapted for night-fighting duties), took up residence. The tenure was short-lived: No 44 disbanded at the end of 1919, North Weald was henceforth reduced to Care and Maintenance and the site was officially relinquished by the War Office in February the following year. The final Officer Commanding was Major A. T. Harris, who, as Sir Arthur 'Bomber' Harris, was to become one of our greatest World War II leaders as C-in-C RAF Bomber Command.

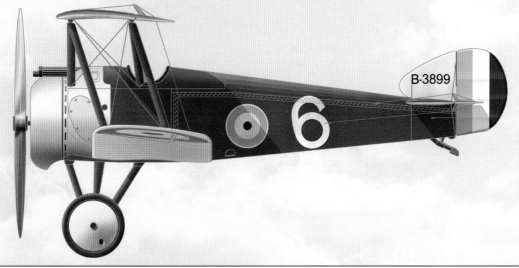

B-3899

Right: Not all No 44 Squadron's Camels were modified for night fighting: this photograph shows one of its aircraft in the original form, its twin Vickers guns mounted over the front fuselage and synchronised to fire through the propeller

ON SILVER WINGS

AS is the habit in our history, the end of hostilities in Europe in 1918 led to massive reductions in the strength of our armed forces—not least in the newly named Royal Air Force: the number of front-line squadrons, which at the close of World War I stood at 188, was reduced to a mere 25. North Weald was to suffer the consequences, and by the end of 1919 it had lost its aircraft, the airfield returning to its pastoral heritage of grazing cattle. The mid-1920s were to see a revival, however, as, under the iconic leadership of Air Marshal Sir Hugh Trenchard, the RAF began to regain some of its teeth.

The redevelopment of the airfield began in 1926 and was completed in September 1927 when, under the command of Wing Commander A. G. R. Garrod MC DFC, North Weald reopened as a fighter station. Aeroplane accommodation took the form of two 'A' type hangars, although the runways were still mown grass (and would remain thus for many more years). As with many of the rebuilt RAF airfields, the hangars were spaced to allow the construction of a third, in between, if such were demanded in the future. New quarters and facilities were constructed, sited in the south-east corner of the airfield and across the main road.

On 11 October 1927 the Armstrong-Whitworth Siskin Mk IIIs of No 56 (Fighter) Squadron flew the short distance from Biggin Hill in Kent to become the first unit to take up permanent residence at the newly refurbished aerodrome. Led by Squadron Leader C. H. Elliott-Smith AFC, the Squadron brought with it a legacy of World War I accolades, including the spirits of two famous 'aces', Captains Albert Ball and James Thomas Byford McCudden, whose personal achievements—and medal-count— are the stuff of legend. Among the new pilots of No 56 Squadron was a

No 56 (F) Squadron

Motto
Quid si Cœlum Ruat
('What if Heaven Falls?')

Equipment
Armstrong Whitworth Siskin Mk IIIA (1927–1932), Bristol Bulldog Mk IIA (1932–1936), Gloster Gauntlet Mk II (1936–1937), Gloster Gladiator Mk I (1937–1938), Hawker Hurricane Mk I (1938–1941), Hawker Hurricane Mk IIB (1941)

Below: A No 56 Squadron Siskin pilot prepares to take off. The aircraft, J9895, carries the individual identity letter 'D' in red just behind the engine. The Squadron hangar is in the background.

Right: A profile of a Siskin Mk IIIA wearing the red and white chequerboard markings of No 56 Squadron. The Siskin was unusual in that the entire tail assembly—vertical fin and rudder and horizontal tail-plane—moved in unison to facilitate control in the air. In about 1930, the rudder striping on RAF aeroplanes was altered, from blue foward to red forward. Siskins carried their underside wing roundels beneath the upper mainplane rather than the considerably smaller lower mainplane.

ARMSTRONG WHITWORTH SISKIN Mk IIIA
Type: Fighter
Engine: One 385hp Armstrong Siddeley Jaguar IVs radial
Length: 25ft 4in (7.72m)
Wing span: 33ft 2in (10.11m)
Speed: 153mph (246kph) max.
Endurance: 2–3hrs
Armament: Two fixed Vickers 0.303in machine guns (1,200rds total) plus up to four 20lb (9kg) bombs
Crew: Pilot only

certain Flying Officer T. G. Pike, whose name was later to become almost synonymous with that of North Weald.

Public interest in flying, born before and matured during World War I, continued after the hostilities had ceased, and was nurtured by air shows

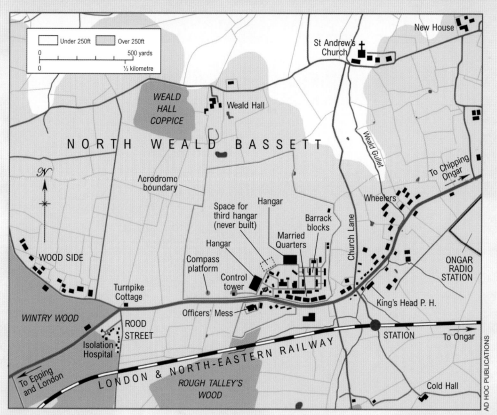

COURTESY PHILIP JARRETT

Above, right: Three red 'Xs' pro-claim No 29 Squadron, the second front-line fighter unit to be headquartered at North Weald after World War I, and on this Siskin the Squadron emblem is carried on the tailfin as well. The aircraft is fitted with a camera gun centrally on the top wing.

Right: The layout of the airfield in the late 1920s, showing the two A type hangars, angled away from each other so as to minimise damage in the event of an enemy bombing raid. A multitude of permanent structures for servicing the aircraft and housing the personnel now occupies the south-eastern corner of the airfield, whose overall dimensions are, however, not much enlarged from ten years previously. Off to the east, Ongar Radio Station has appeared.

AD HOC PUBLICATIONS

COURTESY NWAM

COURTESY PHILIP JARRETT

Left, upper: No 56's officers and airmen pose for a formal photograph with one of their Siskins shortly after the Squadron's arrival at North Weald. The officer standing immediately in front of the aircraft's engine is Flying Officer Thomas Pike.

Left, lower: No 29 Squadron flying over the Essex countryside. The unit markings were carried across the span of the upper wing as well as on the fuselage sides.

Right, upper: Personnel of No 29 Squadron and one of their aircraft in front of their hangar at North Weald.

No 29 Squadron

Motto
Impiger et Acer
('Energetic and Keen')

Equipment
Armstrong Whitworth Siskin Mk IIIA (1928–1932), Bristol Bulldog Mk IIA (1932–1935), Hawker Demon (1935–1936, 1936–1937)

Above: A No 29 Squadron flight sergeant checks the wireless equipment in a Siskin.
Above, right: A Siskin Mk IIIA in the colours of No 29 Squadron.
Below: No 29 Squadron's Siskins at Hendon; the aeroplanes of sister-unit No 56 are paraded in front of them.

such as the famous Annual Pageants held at RAF Hendon in what is now north London. No 56 Squadron, commanded by Squadron Leader A. Lees AFC, was one of the units flying formation displays there in March 1929—not, perhaps, the best time of year in which to hold such an event!

Joining North Weald shortly after No 56's arrival was a second fighter squadron, No 29, which landed from Duxford in Cambridgeshire to take up residence on 1 April 1928, under the command of Squadron Leader M. L. Taylor AFC. These were the heady days of Empire, which saw the

country hosting innumerable visiting Royal and high-ranking foreign VIPs, and on a number of occasions it fell to the two North Weald squadrons to demonstrate their prowess as pilots in front of the dignitaries, conducting displays which served not only to impress the invited guests but also, perhaps, to remind smaller nations that they should not step out of line!

Above: No 29 Squadron's Siskins thrill the crowds at one of the hugely popular Hendon Pageants.

Prowess in the air has always been honed in the Royal Air Force by means of inter-unit competition and rivalry, and in the 1930s this was well to the fore, both between No 29 and 56 Squadrons and amongst the RAF's fighter squadrons generally. Navigation—in those days carried out solely by means of maps and 'dead reckoning'—featured very highly, with map-reading and 'pinpointing' trophies being competed for with a great degree of success by the North Weald squadrons. There was a significant occurrence at the end of May 1929—the first ever fitting of radio telephones to squadron aircraft. Reflecting on the Hendon Air Pageants, with the realisation that they were carried out without the aid of air-to-ground communications, it seems amazing that the pilots taking part were able to perform in the spectacular way that they did.

Above: Squadron Leader G. E. Wilson, OC No 56 Squadron, flew this Bulldog, the rudder specially marked with his rank pennant and with the Squadron emblem, a phœnix rising, within one of the fin chequers.
Below: No 29 Squadron's Bulldogs at North Weald, with their unit markings applied. The aircraft still have tailskids, and note, too, that hardened taxiways are now in evidence—something of an incompatibility!

The year 1932 saw both squadrons re-equip with the more capable Bristol Bulldog fighter and, again, entertain the crowds at the Hendon show, led on this occasion by the North Weald Station Commander. While the Siskin was the first all-metal-framed aeroplane to become standard equipment for the RAF, the Bulldog offered a big improvement in terms of speed, sturdiness and aerodynamic

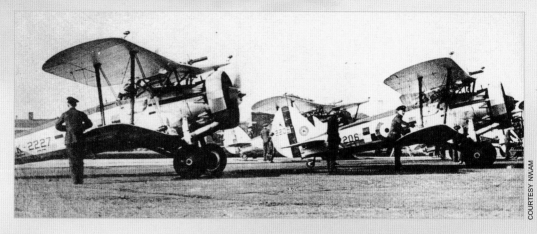

Right: Illustrating the non-standard cowling ring that was fitted to many of the unit's Bulldogs—principally in the interests of reducing drag—this photograph depicts No 56 Squadron's aircraft. The broad-chord tailfin that was later fitted to Bulldogs in order to improve the aeroplane's directional stability, and the castoring tailwheel that replaced the original tailskid, are also evident

COURTESY IWAM

refinement. It narrowly beat its main competitor, the Hawker Hawfinch, as a replacement for the Siskin, principally owing to its more straight-forward demands in terms of maintenance. North Weald pilots were amongst those who carried out trials on the aircraft when prototype Bull-dogs were tested there as early as the spring of 1928.

Right: A photograph taken in June 1932, the month in which No 29 Squadron exchanged its Siskins for Bulldogs. Here two of the new aircraft, their unit markings not yet applied, flank Siskin J8651, which sports a fetching Squadron emblem—an eagle attacking a buzzard—on its tailfin. A second Siskin is parked forward.

COURTESY PHILIP JARRETT

BRISTOL BULLDOG Mk IIA
Type: Fighter
Engine: One 440hp Bristol Jupiter VIIF radial
Length: 25ft 2in (7.67m)
Wing span: 33ft 10in (10.31m)
All-up weight: 3,530lb (1,600kg)
Speed: 178mph (287kph) max.
Ceiling: 29,300ft (8,930m)
Armament: Two fixed Vickers 0.303in machine guns, plus up to four 20lb (9kg) bombs
Crew: Pilot only

Above: A profile of a Bristol Bulldog IIA of No 29 Squadron. The fuselage top-decking was finished in dark olive green—helping to reduce glare for the pilot. As with their Siskins, both squadrons displayed their unit markings across the span of the upper wing .

COURTESY PHILIP JARRETT

Left: Flying accidents were an unfortunate way of life at prewar North Weald. Bulldog K2198 (centre) of No 29 Squadron, manned by Pilot Officer Devas, ended a flight upside down in 1932.

COURTESY PHILIP JARRETT

Left: Bulldog K2200 (top) folded in half during an emergency landing in April 1933, its Jupiter engine finishing up alongside the tailfin. Happily, the pilot, Flying Officer Hobson of No 29 Squadron, was not badly injured. Notice the camera gun atop the upper wing. Neighbouring villagers are taking a keen interest, along with couple of schoolboys and the local constabulary.

COURTESY PHILIP JARRETT

Left: K2154 was written off after crashing in a muddy field. There is evidence of serious fire damage, and the airframe is almost entirely stripped of its canvas, but neither the name of the pilot nor his fate can be established. No 29 Squadron's insignia can be seen on the tailfin.

With the rearmament of Germany starting to become common knowledge, public interest remained high in the goings-on 'over the fence', and this fascination led to the decision to hold the first Empire Air Day at North Weald on 24 May 1934, when a large crowd—for those days—of some 3,000 people came to view the nation's 'teeth' in action. This event, which became an annual fixture until the last was held on 20 May 1939, offered visitors a degree of access to the RAF stations around the country that today's enthusiasts can only dream about as the intimate, day-to-day workings of the Service were revealed for all to see—as demonstrated by the 'Tour of the Station' provided in North Weald's official Empire Air Day programme for 29 May 1937 (see opposite).

Right: A profile illustrating No 56 Squadron's Bulldog IIA K2206, which sports the experimental cowling fitted to some of the unit's aircraft. The new tailwheel is also fitted, and notice, too, the redesigned, broader-chord tailfin characteristic of later Bulldogs.

A Tour of the Station, 1937

'Members of the Public are invited to visit various departments of the Station and to see for themselves how we live and how our work is carried out.

'Visitors are particularly requested to move as quickly as possible through the various buildings in order that those following may not be unduly delayed.

'Service personnel will be available in every building to explain the equipment on view and to answer questions . . .

'**Guard Room.** This consists of the sleeping quarters and living room of the R.A.F. Service Police; the detention room, cells, exercise yard, ablution, etc.

'**Aeroplane Repair Section.** Complete overhauls to airframes are carried out here. (An airframe is an aeroplane without its engine).

'**Carpenters' Shop.**

'**Basic Training Centre.** This is where the training received by an airman as an apprentice is furthered to fit him for promotion and to maintain his skill of hand.

'**Miniature Rifle Range.** The Fighting Area Miniature Rifle Shooting Cup has been won by teams from this Station for the last two years.

'**Educational Class Rooms.** Here, under a qualified education officer, personnel are taught up to a level approximately to intermediate standard for a degree at a British University.

'**Engine Repair Section.** Complete overhauls to the aero engines in use at this Station are carried out here. Engines are then run on the test bench until passed out as ready for installing in an airframe by the Technical Warrant officer.

'**Coppersmiths' Shop.**

'**Blacksmiths' Shop.**

'**Parachute Section.** All parachutes are normally opened, aired and re-packed once a month. There are always a certain number hanging up for inspection and airing.

'**Armoury.** All repairs to machine-guns and firearms generally are carried out here. Examples of machine-guns, interruptor gear and camera guns are on view. The spare anti-gas respirator store is situated here.

'**Watch Office.** This is the office of the Duty Pilot and the Airman of the Watch. It is being used by the Officer in charge of Flying Events to-day.

'**Fire Tender Garage.** Whenever flying is in progress, the fire tender with its crew is situated here, ready to proceed to a crash at a moment's notice.

'**Stop Butts.** This is where the machine-guns of every aircraft are tested periodically. A red flag is hoisted just prior to firing.

'**Main Station Stores.** Equipment of every description is received from the various Depots into Main Stores, where it is taken on to Station charge and reissued as and when required.

'**Fire Section.** The Fire Tender is housed here when no flying is in progress and the fire picquet sleeps in the adjoining room during its tour of duty.

'**Transport Yard.** All vehicles, except the Fire Tender and Petrol Tankers, are housed here.

'**Barrack Blocks.** Airmen sleep 16 in each room, and there are four rooms in each block. One ground floor room is open for inspection. Here will be seen the airmen's lockers, beds and bedding. One complete kit will be laid out for inspection. Non-commissioned Officers have separate rooms. Lavatories, baths, showers and drying rooms are provided in each block.

'**Sergeants' Mess.** This consists of a hall, billiards room, games room, ante room, and dining room; besides bar, kitchen, etc. All Warrant Officers, Flight Sergeants and Sergeants are members of the Mess.

'**Institute.** This is managed by the Navy, Army and Air Force Institute. The profits of this concern return to the above Services in some form or another and are used for their welfare and amusement. The rooms provided include:–

'(i) Restaurant: where the airmen can obtain tea, cakes, fruit, soft drinks, cigarettes and hot suppers at a very reasonable cost.

'(ii) Wet Bar: where beer, etc., is sold.

'(iii) Billiards Room, with two tables, which are in constant demand.

'(iv) Library: containing 2,500 books. On an average there are 150 books on loan, at 1d. each per week.

'(v) Reading and Writing Rooms.

'(vi) Games Room: where table tennis and darts are played.

'(vii) Corporals' Club: consisting of a sitting room and a games room. This Club is run by a committee of Corporals.

'(viii) A Grocery Bar: which provides anything that may be required in the shape of groceries, and is a source of convenience to the officers' and airmen's married families.

'**Sick Quarters.** This is a miniature hospital, complete with operating theatre, consulting room, dispensary, public and private wards and dental surgery. It is supervised by Officers of the Royal Air Force Medical and Dental Services.

'**Church.** This is one of the ordinary barrack rooms converted into a church, where divine service is held every Sunday.

'**Ration Store.** This building contains the butcher's shop, the bread and ration store, and, at the far end, is the barber's shop.

'**Dining Hall & Cookhouse.** The Dining Hall, together with its wooden annexe, is capable of seating comfortably 200 airmen. Here all the single Corporals and Aircraftmen have their meals. These consist of Breakfast, Dinner and Tea, and Supper on four evenings of the week. It is at the wish of the Airmen themselves that suppers are only served on Mondays, Tuesdays, Wednesdays and Thursdays. . . . One week's rations for one airman are laid out for inspection. The Dining Hall is also used for concerts and dances at frequent intervals. An electric washer-up is installed in the scullery and an electric potato peeler in one of the outhouses. A boiler supplies steam to the steamers, hot plates and electric washer; and ample ranges are provided in the cookhouse. A fish-frying apparatus is also installed.

'**Flight Hangars.** Here the aircraft are housed and worked upon. The various annexes around the hangars consist of Squadron and Flight Commanders' offices, Squadron Adjutant's and Clerks' offices, Pilots' and Aircraft Crews' rest rooms, stores and workshops.

'**Pilots' Locker Rooms.** These buildings are fitted up with steel cupboards, wherein each pilot keeps his flying clothing and parachute.'

The mid-1930s brought significant changes to the Station as it became clear that a new threat loomed in continental Europe, and the measures to meet it began to be put into place. The Siskins had flown from North Weald for five years and the Bulldogs were resident for four, but between 1935 and 1939 no fewer than four different aircraft types, of rapidly increasing capability, were introduced into service, marking as they did the transition from the two-gun biplane fighter to the eight-gun monoplane fighter. Hand in hand with these improvements in equipment went ever-increasing numbers of resident aircraft and upgraded facilities, including the building of hard runways to supplement the verdant take-off and landing strips that had characterised the airfield hitherto. The comparatively carefree flying days were swiftly coming to an end: more serious business might well have to be addressed.

The first of the two squadrons to lose its Bulldogs was No 29, which in March 1935 took delivery of replacements in the form of Hawker Demons. These elegant biplanes, developed directly from the Hart bomber—a remarkable machine which caused a stir when it first appeared in 1930 not only for its futuristic streamlining but also, and

Above: A trio of No 29 Squadron Demons, their gunners' attention attracted by events off to port,

HAWKER DEMON
Type: Fighter
Engine: One 485hp Rolls-Royce Kestrel IIS (Turret Demon 584hp Kestrel VDR) inline
Length: 29ft 7in (9.02m)
Wing span: 37ft 2in (11.33m)
Speed: 182mph (293kph) max.
Ceiling: 24,500ft (7,470m)
Armament: Two fixed Vickers Mk III 0.303in machine guns (600rds), plus one movable 0.303in Lewis machine gun (582rds)
Crew: Pilot and gunner

Right: The sleek Hawker Demon brought a new shape of aeroplane to the squadrons at North Weald—and, for the first time, inline, water-cooled engines. This profile depicts a Demon of No 29 Squadron, the yellow fin and wheels denoting a flight leader's aircraft.

Right: The introduction of a turret improved the Demon gunner's effectiveness if not the aircraft's æsthetics. No 29 Squadron's commission at North Weald was interrupted by an eleven-month deployment to the Middle East.

GLOSTER GAUNTLET Mk II
Type: Fighter
Engine: One 640hp Bristol Mercury VIS2 radial
Length: 26ft 5in (8.05m)
Wing span: 32ft 9½in (9.99m)
Weight: 2,770lb (1,255kg) empty, 3,970lb (1,800kg) loaded
Speed: 230mph (370kph) max.
Ceiling: 33,500ft (10,210m)
Armament: Two fixed Vickers Mk III 0.303in machine guns (1,200rds)
Crew: Pilot only

Left: A turret Demon serving with No 29 Squadron. Lacking fuselage and wing-top decoration, this aircraft displays its squadron allegiance only by means of the emblem on the tailfin, with a Squadron Leader's pennant above it.
Right: A flight of Gloster Gauntlets of No 56 Squadron begins to peel off. Silver wings were still filling the skies around North Weald—but their days were numbered.

more significantly, because it outpaced the fighters then in service—marked a reversion to the two-seat formula that had found favour in fighter aircraft of World War I, with a gunner positioned in a second cockpit behind the pilot, armed with a swivelling machine gun to supplement the two fixed, forward-firing Vickers guns.

Impressive though it was, the aircraft had its problems, one being the exposure to the slipstream of the gunner attempting to operate his Lewis gun at speeds in excess of 150mph. In an effort to make his life more comfortable, a rotating turret incorporating a segmented windshield ('lobster-back') was introduced to the rear cockpit, and this became a feature of later aircraft.

Within six months of receiving its new aircraft, however, No 29 Squadron departed for Egypt on 4 October 1935 to help deal with the crisis developing as a result of Mussolini's ambitions in East Africa. It would return in the summer of the following year. Meanwhile, in May 1936, No 56 Squadron began to replace its Bulldogs with a different type of aircraft—single-seat Gloster Gauntlets.

COURTESY PHILIP JARRETT

In the Gauntlet, the RAF had for the first time a 200mph-plus fighter aircraft, and the interceptor biplane was reaching its most advanced form of development. Impressive though its top speed was, however, the pilot was beginning to suffer the rigours of an open cockpit at such velocities—especially in the winter months when there were freezing temperatures to contend with also—and many questioned whether his combat efficiency was now beginning to be degraded.

No 56 Squadron had the airfield much to itself during the autumn, winter and spring of 1935–36 while its long-time rivals were away in warmer climes, but in August 1936 the gap was filled by forming a separate unit out of the Squadron's 'B' Flight of 56 Squadron—a move typical of the expansion being seen all over the country in the second half of the 1930s. Equipped, like its parent, with Gauntlets, the new unit took up the 'nameplate' of No 151 Squadron, which had last seen life flying Sopwith Camels in France during World War I—and, perhaps not uncoincidentally, had a tangible North Weald connection since it had originally been commissioned at nearby Hainault Farm in 1918 and its pilots at that time would have been very familiar with the airfield.

No 151 (F) Squadron

Motto
Foy pour Devoir
('Fidelity for Duty')

Equipment
Gloster Gauntlet Mk II (1936–1939), Hawker Hurricane Mk I (1938–1940)

Above, left: Gloster Gauntlet Mk II K5288 in the colours of No 56 Squadron, 1936.

COURTESY PHILIP JARRETT

Left: On 4 August 1936 No 151 (F) Squadron was re-formed at North Weald from a detachment of No 56 Squadron and three of the original Gauntlets are seen here at the airfield. The red and white chequerboard markings have been erased but the new colours have yet to be applied.

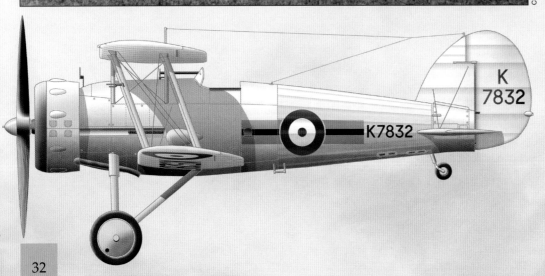

Left: A profile of Gauntlet Mk II K7832, showing the colours of No 151 Squadron.

Above: Flying with the Gauntlets. Notice how, on K5300, the design of the red and white No 56 Squadron chequerboard has been compromised by what is probably anodising of the metal panelling around the pilot's entry footholds.

Above: The gunner's position in a Hawker Turret Demon, the 'lobster back' protection clearly visible.

Right: Gauntlets of No 151 Squadron lined up and chocked at North Weald. Again, the metal fuselage cladding of the nearest aircraft is considerably darker in shade than the fabric-covered areas of the airframe. The next aircraft along, K7890, has had its engine cowling similarly treated.

As the rearmament programme got under way, North Weald started to become a much busier place as, within a few weeks, in October 1936, No 29 returned with their Demons, and—having flown Fairey Gordon bombers (!) for a brief period while out east—they continued to fly the Hawker two-seaters for another year. Doubtless what one would nowadays call 'dissimilar combat training' took place from time to time!

From the summer of 1937 it seemed that changes were taking place at North Weald every few weeks. First, in July, No 56 Squadron's aircrew began to relinquish their Gauntlets in favour of its improved successor the Gloster Gladiator, similar in general configuration but with a more potent engine, the novelty of a fully enclosed cockpit for the pilot, more stream-lining in the shape of fewer interplane struts and cantilevered main undercarriage struts, and four instead of two machine guns, the extra pair in faired housings beneath the lower wing—and, as a result all of these changes, faster and with twice the firepower. Then, on the 30th of the month, the aerodrome became more a good deal more crowded when No 64 Squadron, *en masse*, flew its Hawker Demons in from Martlesham Heath—although they stayed for a mere two weeks before returning to Suffolk. Further major reorganisation came on 22 November 1937, when No 29 Squadron, whose silver biplanes had been so familiar to the local population, left North Weald for the very last time to take up residence at

Left: The Gauntlets of No 56 Squadron, chocked and lined up at North Weald in the winter of 1937/38. The pilot's gun sight is clearly seen on the nearest aircraft, projecting from the windscreen. Notice the individual identity letters carried above the gun troughs—which latter, it is believed, were finished in red on No 56's machines.

Debden a little further to the north, severing an intimate connection with the airfield that had endured for ten years.

Then, in March the following year, a revolutionary new shape was seen in the skies above the airfield with the arrival, for No 56 Squadron, of the first Hawker Hurricanes. In a single aircraft design, staggered biplane wings, struts, fixed undercarriages, flying wires, rigging wires and machine guns firing through propellers had been abolished at a stroke,

Below, left: No 56 Squadron's officers and airmen pose proudly at the front of their hangar with a Gladiator, August 1937—the aircraft easily distinguishable from the Gauntlet in this view by dint of the absence of inboard inter-plane wing struts.

GLOSTER GLADIATOR Mk I
Type: Fighter
Engine: One 830hp Bristol Mercury IX radial
Length: 27ft 5in (8.36m)
Wing span: 32ft 3in (9.83m)
Weight: 3,220lb (1,460kg) empty, 4,595lb (2,085kg) loaded
Speed: 253mph (407kph) max.
Ceiling: 32,800ft (10,000m)
Armament: Two fixed Browning and two fixed Vickers (or four fixed Browning) 0.303in machine guns
Crew: Pilot only

Left: A Gladiator in the colours of No 56 Squadron. The Gladiator was the first RAF's four-gun fighter and the first with an enclosed cockpit—and it was the last biplane to serve in Fighter Command.

Right: No 151's Gauntlets on parade at North Weald. As with No 56's aircraft, the Squadron colours appeared large across the span of the upper wing. Although all these aircraft are Mk IIs, both two- and three-blade propellers are evident. The circular area of hardstanding visible in the top of the photograph is the compass swinging platform, which was located close to the Epping–Ongar road.

Below: A No 56 Squadron Gladiator prepares to fly from North Weald.

AD HOC COLLECTION

and instead was a sleek, purposeful-looking monoplane accompanied by the distinctive roar of a Rolls-Royce Merlin engine. Gone, too, were the bright silver finishes and the garish squadron markings, replaced by sombre camouflage in browns and greens and, perhaps, a miniature unit emblem restricted to the tailfin. It was a harbinger of things to come.

No 56 Squadron was the third RAF fighter squadron to equip with the type, and in December 1938 No 151 Squadron bid farewell to its Gauntlets as it, too, took delivery of the new aircraft. The Hurricane was the first low-wing monoplane with a retractable undercarriage. Its construction of metal framing and, for the most part, fabric skinning allowed for rapid production and facilitated battle-damage repair—both essential requisites for a fighter aircraft that was to bear the brunt of the early years of the European war that by this time was seeming inevitable. The Hawker lineage was evident in the shape and design, and the colossal leap in performance can be appreciated by comparing the Hurricane's performance figures with those of the Demon. Some 500 examples were in service by September 1939, equipping eighteen Fighter Command squadrons. The Hurricane was to go on to become the legendary aircraft of World War II that we all remember today, and the fighter with which North Weald will always be associated.

HAWKER HURRICANE Mk I
Type: Fighter
Engine: One 1,030hp Rolls-Royce Merlin II or III inline
Length: 31ft 5in (9.58m)
Wing span: 40ft 0in (12.19m)
Weight: 4,670lb (2,120kg) empty, 6,600lb (2,995kg) loaded
Speed: 320mph (515kph) max.
Ceiling: 33,400ft (10,200m)
Range: 440 miles (710km)
Armament: Eight fixed Browning 0.303in machine guns
Crew: Pilot only

Right: Hurricane Mk I 'C' of No 56 Squadron. This is an early-production aircraft, with two-blade propeller and retractable tailwheel.

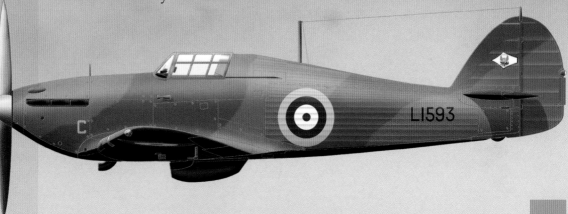

Empire Air Day

FLYING PROGRAMME

EMPIRE AIR DAY - 1937

ROYAL AIR FORCE STATION, NORTH WEALD

Event No.	Time p.m.		Aircraft.	Squadron.
1.	2.30.	Individual Aerobatics.	1 Gauntlet.	151.
2.	2.40.	Flight Drill.	5 Gauntlets.	56.
3.	2.55.	Dive-bombing attack on aerodrome.	3 Hinds.	Visiting Squadron.
4.	3.00.	Flight attack on bombing raid, followed by refuelling and re-arming of Fighters.	3 Gauntlets. 3 Hinds.	151. Visiting Squadron.
5.	3.20.	Anti-gas Demonstration.	1 Demon.	29.
6.	3.30.	Attack on towed target.	Gauntlets.	56.
7.	3.40.	Individual Aerobatics.	1 Gauntlet.	151.
8.	3.50.	Height Judging Competition.	1 Gauntlet.	151.
	4.00.	TEA INTERVAL.		

During the interval, members of the Woodford Model Aero Club will give an exhibition of model flying.

Event No.	Time p.m.		Aircraft.	Squadron.
9.	5.00.	Individual Aerobatics.	1 Gauntlet.	151.
10.	5.10.	Flight Drill.	5 Gauntlets.	56.
11.	5.25.	Anti-gas Demonstration.	1 Demon.	29.
12.	5.35.	Flight attack on bombing raid followed by re-fuelling and re-arming of fighters.	3 Gauntlets. 3 Hinds.	151. Visiting Squadron.
13.	5.55.	Message picking up and supply dropping by parachute.	1 Audax.	4.
14.	6.05.	Individual Aerobatics.	1 Gauntlet.	151.
15.	6.15.	All Squadrons and aircraft take off and fly past in succession.		
16.	6.30.	Cease Flying.		

NOTE: This programme is liable to modification or curtailment according to weather conditions.

The Performing Right Society Limited and Phonograph Performance Limited have kindly agreed, on the payment of a nominal sum as recognition of their rights, that copyright music from their repertoire may be broadcast by loud-speakers at this station to-day.

Left: The Flying Programme for the 1937 Empire Air Day at RAF North Weald.
Below: The covers of two Empire Air Day Official Programmes, 1937 and 1939.
Bottom: Close inspection of a No 17 Squadron Gloster Gauntlet by both servicemen and members of the public— with the aircraft's engine running. Empire Air Day, North Weald, 1937.

ROYAL AIR FORCE
OFFICIAL PROGRAMME
6ᴰ
EMPIRE AIR DAY
MAY 29ᵀᴴ 1937

EMPIRE AIR DAY
6ᴰ OFFICIAL PROGRAMME 6ᴰ
ROYAL AIR FORCE

COURTESY PHILIP JARRETT

PARTICIPATING AIRCRAFT, EMPIRE AIR DAY, RAF NORTH WEALD, SATURDAY 29 MAY 1937

Gloster Gauntlets K5287, K5289, K5291, K5295, K5296, K5300 and K7807 (all No 56 Squadron), K5351, K5352, K5353, K5354, K5364, K7831, K7832, K7833, K7841, K7866, K7867, K7869, K7873, K7890 and K7890 (all No 151 Squadron) and five further unidentified Gauntlets, Avro Anson K6277, Hawker Audax K3689 (No IV Squadron), Hawker Demons K2843, K3766, K3782, K5136 (all No 29 Squadron) and one other unidentified Demon, D. H.

Dragonfly G-AEDT, Hawker Fury K8255, Fairey Gordons K1160 and K1747, Hawker Hart K3???, Hart Trainer K6465 (No 56 squadron) and Hart Trainer K6847, H. P. Heyford K4392, Hawker Hinds K5415, K5432 and K5460 (all No XV Squadron), D. H. Leopard Moth G-ACUK, D. H. Moth K1894, D. H. Rapides G-ADFX and G-AERE, Blackburn Shark K4361, D. H. Tiger Moths K4246 and K6244, Avro Tutor K3409

No 17 (F) Squadron

Motto
Excellere Contende
('Strive to Excel')

Equipment
Gloster Gauntlet Mk II (1939),
Hawker Hurricane Mk I (1939)

Right, top: Gloster Gauntlets of No 17 (F) Squadron, which took up residence at North Weald in the spring of 1939. A year earlier, the Munich Crisis had dictated that they be camouflaged in preparation for the conflict that weekly seemed likely. The aircraft nearest the camera has the code letters 'UV' crudely painted in dull red forward of the fuselage roundel, although it is not possible to make out the individual aircraft code letter.

Right, upper: Code letters came to be more or less standardised in light grey during 1939, as shown in this profile of a Gauntlet of No 17 Squadron—although it is not known whether all of the unit's Gauntlets were so modified. The serial number of the aircraft depicted in this profile was, for a period at least, obliterated.

Right: By June 1939 No 17 Squadron was flying early-production Hurricanes, one of which is shown in this profile.

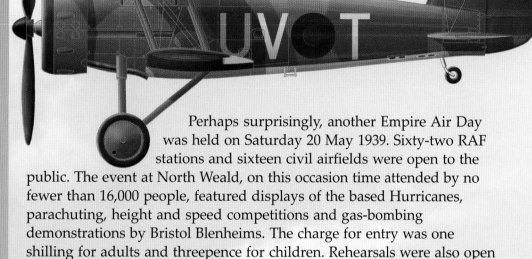

Perhaps surprisingly, another Empire Air Day was held on Saturday 20 May 1939. Sixty-two RAF stations and sixteen civil airfields were open to the public. The event at North Weald, on this occasion time attended by no fewer than 16,000 people, featured displays of the based Hurricanes, parachuting, height and speed competitions and gas-bombing demonstrations by Bristol Blenheims. The charge for entry was one shilling for adults and threepence for children. Rehearsals were also open to the public.

That month had witnessed the arrival of another fighter squadron at North Weald when No 17 had flown in with its Gauntlets, having spent the previous five years at RAF Kenley in Surrey. Almost immediately it began converting to Hurricanes, and by the end of June it had become the third front-line Hurricane squadron at the Essex airfield, joining Nos 56 and 151.

It was at about this time that a new system of identifying the units to which aircraft belonged came into force. The colourful squadron *décor* and unit emblems had been banished, and in their place came a three-letter code system, the first two identifying the squadron and the last the individual aircraft. No 17 Squadron were allocated the letters 'UV', No 56 'LR' and No 151 'DZ' although No 17's were quickly changed to 'YB' and No 56's to 'US'.

Meanwhile, away from the public gaze, preparations for war were in full swing . . .

THE FINEST HOUR

IN order to meet the widely expected eventual onslaught against the British Isles by the German Luftwaffe, radical changes to the structure of the Royal Air Force had taken place during the years up to 1939. For the purposes of administration and efficient organisation, Fighter Command had been divided into 'Groups', each with a command head-quarters and each subdivided into sub-groups called 'Sectors'. North Weald was the most important airfield within 'E' Sector, and, along with the other component sectors of No 11 Group, had for the second time in its history the primary task of defending the capital. As the conflict developed, it would become the norm to move squadrons around from place to place for rest and aircraft maintenance, and by the time hostilities were over a phenomenal forty-six operational units involving seven Allied nations would have seen service at North Weald.

RAF North Weald was placed on War Alert in August 1938 as a result of the Munich Crisis. On 2 September 1939, the day before war was declared on Germany, No 17 Squadron, having recently been re-equipped with, and worked up on, Hurricanes, departed for RAF Debden, stopping for a week at Croydon en route, but the Station's two remaining squadrons, Nos 56 and 151, were that same day joined from RAF Hendon by No 604 (County of Middlesex) Squadron with its Blenheim Mk IF twin-engine fighters. These aircraft, originally designed as fast light bombers, were among the 200 or so converted prior to delivery to the RAF by having a pack containing four machine guns bolted beneath the

Above: The distinction of making the RAF's very first aerial 'kill' of World War II fell to Flying Officer Richard Milne of No 151 Squadron, who, following a report received at 12 noon on 3 September 1939 that a balloon had been sighted over North Weald, took off in Hurricane L1758 and shot it down.

Left: Hurricanes of No 151 Squadron (L1746 is nearest) parked along the perimeter track at North Weald. The aircraft are probably freshly delivered (December 1938), as they lack unit code letters. Airfield construction is proceeding apace: the building in the background appears to be a new MT facility.

Left: Bristol Blenheims are refuelled at North Weald, in 1939. When the Munich Crisis changed the prospect of conflict with Germany from a remote possibility to a distinct probability, the RAF had little by way of modern, long-range fighters, nor any with an effective night-flying capability, and the Blenheim light bomber, already in production, seemed to offer a quick solution to both difficulties. The principal modification was the addition of a four-barrel gun pack beneath the fuselage.

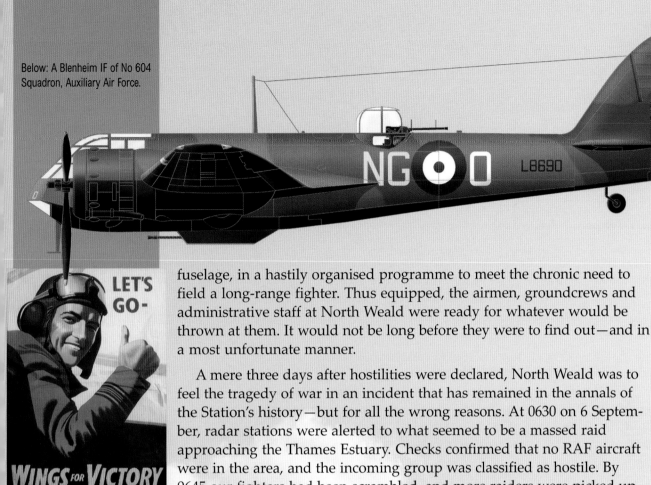

Below: A Blenheim IF of No 604 Squadron, Auxiliary Air Force.

LET'S GO-

WINGS FOR VICTORY

BRISTOL BLENHEIM Mk IF
Type: Long-range fighter
Engine: Two 840hp Bristol Mercury VIII radials
Length: 39ft 9in (12.12m)
Wing span: 56ft 4in (17.17m)
Speed: 260mph (420kph) max.
Range: 920 miles (1,480km) max.
Armament: One fixed Browning 0.202in machine gun and one turret-mounted Vickers 'K' machine gun, plus ventral pack comprising four 0.303in Browning machine guns
Crew: Two (pilot and wireless operator/gunner)

Right: A map showing the extent of No 11 Group's area of operations and its component Sectors. RAF Hornchurch, incidentally, was developed from the World War I site at Sutton's Farm, which was referred to in the first section of this book.

fuselage, in a hastily organised programme to meet the chronic need to field a long-range fighter. Thus equipped, the airmen, groundcrews and administrative staff at North Weald were ready for whatever would be thrown at them. It would not be long before they were to find out—and in a most unfortunate manner.

A mere three days after hostilities were declared, North Weald was to feel the tragedy of war in an incident that has remained in the annals of the Station's history—but for all the wrong reasons. At 0630 on 6 September, radar stations were alerted to what seemed to be a massed raid approaching the Thames Estuary. Checks confirmed that no RAF aircraft were in the area, and the incoming group was classified as hostile. By 0645 our fighters had been scrambled, and more raiders were picked up

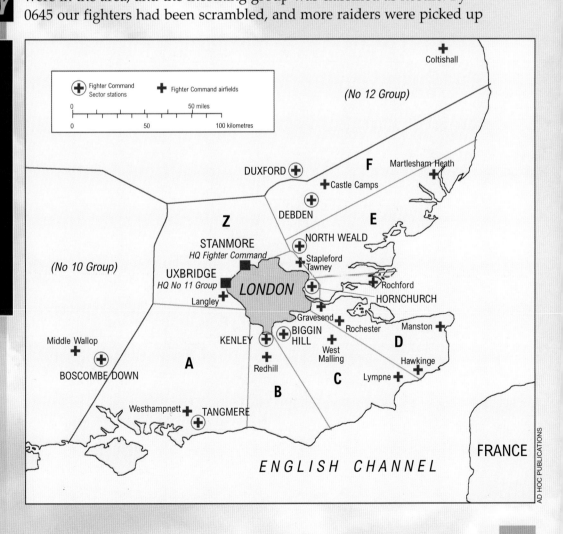

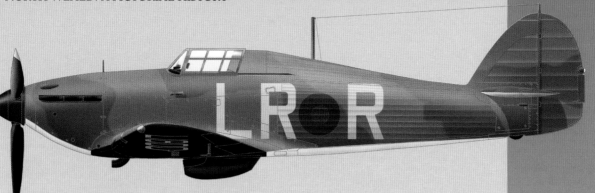

approaching the coast and heading up the Thames. An air-raid warning was issued in the City and sirens were sounded, and before 0700 some seven flights of fighters, all from No 11 Group, were approaching the intruders. No 12 Group were placed on alert, to be scrambled at a moment's notice if necessary.

Anti-aircraft guns were brought into action, and Spitfires from the Hornchurch-based No 74 Squadron joined the fray. The Hurricanes of No 151 Squadron climbed for the sun and were brought into the attack with a warning from their leader, Squadron Leader E. M. Donaldson, to confirm 'identity friend or foe' before engaging. No such warning was given to No 74 Squadron, however. The 'raiders' were quickly identified by Donaldson as Hurricanes, but, despite desperate calls, the Spitfires and the ack-ack continued the attack. The guns hit two RAF fighters, and one Hurricane from No 56 Squadron was seen to glide sedately from the sky, apparently undamaged, and crash to the ground with its pilot, Pilot Officer Montague Hulton-Harrop, still in the cockpit. It is assumed that he had been hit by a bullet and was either killed or unable to control the aircraft.

The returning aircraft crews were irate at the loss of not just the one, but two other Hurricanes resulting from the apparent vectoring of one

Above: As noted, by the time of the outbreak of war, RAF fighter aircraft had been allocated a three-letter coding system, the first two indicating the squadron and the third the individual aircraft within that squadron. No 56's Hurricanes were, as shown in this profile, initially identifiable by the letters 'LR'. For the present, red/blue roundels were specified for the fuselage and upper wing surfaces.

Below: A view looking west-south-west from the top of the southernmost of the two hangars at North Weald in the winter of 1939/40, with Hurricane Mk Is of No 151 Squadron well in evidence. The Isolation Hospital is dimly discernible in the far distance, beyond the new dispersal buildings.

Right; The general layout of North Weald aerodrome just after the outbreak of war in 1939. Preparations for the conflict have radically changed the nature of the site, the considerable extra acreage allowing the construction of a perimeter track around the western side of the airfield, and dispersals away from the two main hangars around the fringes. Hardened runways now feature, although take-offs and landings continued to be made from grassed areas.

Below: Wing Commander F. V. Beamish (right), Station Commander, with Squadron Leader E. M. Donaldson, OC No 151 Squadron, at North Weald, spring 1940.

Bottom: A view from the same vantage point as that opposite, but now looking north-west. Notice the temporary accommodation at far right.

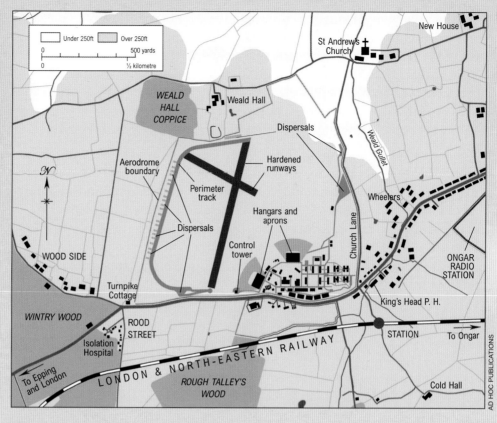

group of friendly aircraft on to another. No reports of any German aircraft were confirmed that day, and Hulton-Harrop became the first pilot to perish in the conflict—albeit at the hands of his own side. Blamed on a technical fault, the disaster occurred because the radar 'blips' of aircraft flying from the west were identified as reflections and therefore as aircraft coming from the east. The more fighters that were scrambled, the greater the mass of raiders appeared.

Unfortunately, this was not to be the only loss in the conflict brought about by friendly fire and, despite the error having originated at the radar station in question (Canewdon, near Southend), the vexed question of 'identification friend or foe' was thereafter accorded the highest priority. Even today, seventy years on, positive identity, enemy or ally, is probably the foremost concern, after personal survival, in the fighter pilot's mind. Hulton-Harrop is buried in St Andrew's churchyard at North Weald.

This incident apart, life at North Weald from September 1939 to January 1940 was in keeping with the 'Phoney War' sobriquet that has since been given to this period of the conflict, Fighter Command's aircraft making little contact with the enemy. Very little action was seen over mainland Britain, and this was primarily a period of reconnaissance and propaganda flights while the build-up of forces proceeded apace in preparation for what was to come. It was at one point planned that No 604 Squadron's Blenheims would be transferred to the Finns, to assist their air force in the 'Winter War' against the Soviet Union, but in the event the Squadron remained intact and moved to RAF Northolt in January 1940. Among the crews of No 604 Squadron was a pilot named John Cunningham who, in later years, with his gunner Jimmy Rawnsley, was to build a great reputation as the highest-scoring night fighter crew: 'Cat's-Eyes' Cunningham was to become a wartime legend.

Meanwhile the British Expeditionary Force, consisting of ten infantry divisions, one tank brigade and 500 aircraft, were positioned in France. Of the North Weald squadrons, No 56 had been detached aircraft to Vitry-en-Artois and No 151 Squadron aircraft were to be found at Vitry and at Abbeville. On 10 May 1940 German troops invaded Belgium, Holland and Luxemburg. France fell, suing for an armistice which came into effect on 25 June, and this led to the withdrawal of the BEF through Dunkirk in the famous evacuation by 'the little ships' known as Operation 'Dynamo'.

North Weald pilots were busy, to say the least, over France in the early summer of 1940: as well as the detachments, home-based aircraft were conducting regular sweeps over the near Continent as the Germans were advancing. Success came to No 151 Squadron on 17 May when six enemy aircraft were shot down and a further three were damaged. As the battle

No 25 Squadron

Motto
Feriens Tego
('Striking, I Defend')

Equipment
Bristol Blenheim Mk IF (1940)

Above: The last resting place of Pilot Officer Montague Hulton-Harrop, at St Andrew's Church, North Weald.
Below: No 56 Squadron's 'LR' code was short-lived and by early 1940 had been replaced by 'US', as on Hurricane Mk I N2479 at North Weald.

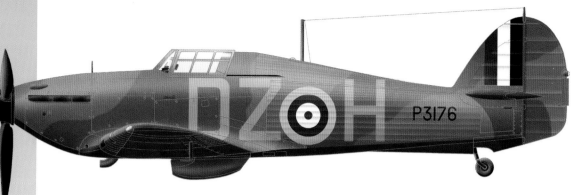

Right: Profile depicting a No 151 Squadron Hurricane Mk I. No 151's aircraft carried the code letters 'DZ' throughout the conflict.

Below: At dispersal: North Weald pilots, living under canvas, Mae Wests donned, waiting . . .

Below: A Blenheim Mk IF of No 25 Squadron, L1257, shortly after arriving at North Weald. In the foreground, armourers are replenishing the ammunition for the starboard wing guns of a Hurricane; the muzzles of the four weapons are visible at the wing leading edge.

turned against the Allies, the Squadron found itself defending the withdrawal from Dunkirk and then patrolling the Thames Estuary. No 56 was also forced to withdraw, this time after four days of raids on its forward base in France; 'B' Flight had been working out of Vitry while 'A' Flight would fly to France for daily missions before returning to Essex overnight. Fourteen Luftwaffe aircraft were accounted for during this period.

June 1940 saw the arrival of a new station commander in the guise of Wing Commander Francis Victor Beamish. Of Irish descent, he was trained at the RAF College at Cranwell, and his reputation as a leader was further enhanced by his spell at North Weald. He had flown with the Royal Canadian Air Force before contracting an illness that invalided him out of the Service and threatened his future career, but he fought his way back to fitness and had returned to flying duties some two years before war broke out. Despite being 37 years of age—positively ancient in terms of fighter pilots—he was to accumulate over 120 sorties during the Battle of Britain and was decorated three times for his successes. He must be listed as amongst the outstanding fighter pilots of the war.

The constant reorganisation of the country's defences led to further comings and goings throughout the spring of 1940. No 604 Squadron had already departed to RAF Northolt on 16 January, to be replaced that same day by No 25 Squadron, also equipped with Bristol Blenheims, in a straight swap. Earlier in the year the nearby general aviation site at Stapleford Tawney had been requisitioned as a satellite airfield for North Weald, and, with new accommodation, improved taxiways and dispersals, was handed over to the RAF in March. On 30 May 1940, as a kind

Then Came Dunkirk . . .

Flight Lieutenant Hal Ironside, pilot, No 151 Squadron

The 18th of May 1940 was the date of our second and last operation from French soil. We landed at a small grass airfield called Vitry near the town of Douai. The only building was a wooden hut which contained a telephone. It would have been better if it had not—as will become clear later. We had not been long settled in when the phone rang. The CO, Squadron Leader Donaldson, answered it and then told us that the HQ had a special mission for us. About noon we discerned aerial activity approaching Douai. The CO immediately got on the phone to HQ and sought permission to attack this large force of enemy aircraft. He was sharply told he was to wait for a briefing on the special mission. Meantime the enemy had reached Douai and was knocking hell out of the town with bombs and cannon fire. The CO tried again but again was met with a curt refusal. When they had finished the task the enemy departed. leaving behind some very frustrated pilots.

A little later we again saw a large formation approaching and again the CO requested in vain that we should intercept. This time the raid did not bomb Douai but came straight for us. As soon as we realised that we were the target we all jumped into a large, deep trench adjacent to the hut. The Me 109s beat up the airfield with cannon and machine guns. Someone had found a French rifle with a full magazine and returned fire. It did no good but it made us feel better.

When the raid was over the CO said, ' To hell with HQ—let's get after them!' The field was shrouded in smoke from burning aircraft but by a miracle none of our squadron's had suffered major damage. Taking off was a hazardous procedure. The smoke made it difficult to see and there were now Me 110s overhead preparing for another attack. Then ensued a vicious dog fight as we climbed up to meet the enemy who was diving down on us. I gave an Me 110 a short burst at full deflection and was amazed to see the entire tail unit part company with the rest of the fuse-lage. I saw a parachute come out but was too busy to watch for more . . .

. . . we were held firmly on the ground by HQ until another raid, this time when Dornier 17 bombers escorted by Me 109s attacked the airfield. Once again we dived for the trench and all hell was let loose around us. As soon as the raiders had gone the CO told us to scramble and form up over the airfield to provide protection in case of another raid. Taking off this time was even more perilous as the field was pitted with bomb craters. Again no aircraft had been damaged and all got off safely. There being no enemy about and all except me being short of fuel, the CO led us back to Manston, the nearest airfield in England. As we left we could see German tanks on the road about a mile from Vitry. We were the last British aircraft to land in France, apart from clandestine operations, for four years.

The following days were hectic. Since we could not land in France we spent a lot of time flying over that country looking for trouble—which we usually found in abundance. In the seven days from the 19th to the 25th of May my logbook records fifteen offensive patrols and bomber escorts over France. The bomber escorts were the most unpopular—we nearly always got bounced off a 'tail end Charlie' as they went after the bombers. In addition to these patrols and escorts, we often had to be at Readiness (i.e., ready to take off in five minutes) half an hour before first light or until last light.

On one scramble we were just too late to prevent some Junkers 88s from bombing a large tanker off Selsey Bill. I was leading the second section two hundred yards behind the CO. One bomb scored a direct hit on the ship: the flames from the explosion—she must have been carrying petrol—appeared to engulf the CO's section for an instant but they escaped unharmed. We chased the 88s but they escaped into cloud, although not before one of them had put a bullet in my propeller. On another occasion we were tasked to protect a damaged cruiser which was under tow in the Channel. It was a difficult job as every time we got near she opened up with every piece of flak she had.

Then came Dunkirk. The Army complained that the RAF failed them at Dunkirk. It was understandable because every time we went there we were involved with superior numbers of Me 109s at high altitude and rarely had

a chance to attack the dive bombers. After nine operations in four days the Squadron was rested for a week. We certainly needed the rest: we were all at the point of exhaustion and had lost several good pilots. One of these was the other flight commander, Ivy Ives, who landed on the beach and by a fluke of atmospherics was able to call North Weald on the radio and tell us that he was safe. Sadly he was lost when the destroyer on which he was returning was sunk. Altogether Fighter Command lost 100 aircraft and 81 pilots at Dunkirk.

After a week we resumed patrolling over France, where the Luftwaffe were busy installing themselves in French airfields all along the coast. We lost one pilot, a New Zealander, who was shot down just off Calais. He was last seen swimming to England. Another time the CO was shot down in mid-Channel by a 109. I watched him leave his blazing aircraft, stand on the wing and fly it towards a small ship until things got too hot then jump and land within a hundred yards of an air–sea rescue launch. He was back in the Mess at North Weald that night.

We frequently operated from forward airfields on the coast so as to give us more time over enemy territory. One day when we were at Tangmere I was briefed by the Intelligence Officer to fly to Cherbourg to find out if it had fallen to the Germans. When asked how I could tell he replied that if the Germans were there they would shoot at me. I remarked that so would the French. He then advised me to see what type of helmet the troops were wearing. I took my Number Two and we set off at nought feet to avoid detection and found Cherbourg without trouble. We spent some ten minutes looking for helmets or other signs of military activity. We found no helmets and no one shot at us. It seemed that the French had departed and the Germans had not yet arrived.

Before long the Germans started seriously to attack convoys in the Channel, so a lot of our time was spent on their protection. On 9 July my flight was ordered to cover a big convoy in the Thames estuary. We had been patrolling for nearly an hour when the controller warned us of an approaching raid, and shortly afterwards my Number Two gave a 'Tally-Ho'. It was an awe-inspiring sight. There were some hundred aircraft stepped up in height from 12,000 to over 20,000 feet. The bombers were at the bottom of the pile, above them the Me110s and above them the 109s. The Station Commander, Victor Beamish, was flying as Yellow Section leader so I told him to break away and try to distract the 109s while I took my section to try to reach the bombers by diving through the 110s. It did not work out: the 109s came down on us like a ton of bricks.

I was attacking a 110 whose gunner was firing back at me when there was a big bang, a blast of air and I was blinded. I instinctively pulled into a steep diving turn and decided that it was a good time to get out. I groped for the handles of the sliding hood, but, try as I might, I could not move it an inch. As I could not get out I had to do a rapid rethink. My eyes were extremely painful as they were full of tiny splinters from the so-called bullet-proof windscreen and the glass of the gun sight. At last I managed to get one eye clear and I pulled out at 2,000 feet in sight of the Essex coast. All my electrics had gone, so when I reached North Weald I flew over the Control Tower with, I hoped, the wheels down. They gave me a green light so I landed and taxied to the hangar. It took some time to prise off the hood as the runners had been damaged, but eventually I was freed and carted off to sick quarters for First Aid and then to hospital. So ended my operational flying. My Number Two, Midshipman Wightman (yes, we were that short of pilots), was shot down and rescued from the sea, sadly to be killed a year later. Yellow Section had claimed a 109.

As a footnote to this marvellous account from the late Hal Ironside, the following remarks are taken from a letter written to him by the late Air Commodore Donaldson in 1990: 'I hope you have forgiven me for the injuries I gave you with the axe when I chopped you out of your Hurricane at North Weald, but with everything soaked in petrol and your hood jammed firmly closed, it seemed the only thing to do.'

Right: A Blenheim Mk IF, 'ZK-P' of No 25 Squadron, photographed from the dorsal turret of a companion Blenheim in April 1940 while operating from North Weald; the position of the underbelly gun pack is clearly visible. These aircraft, as well as providing a night-fighter capability, were engaged in valuable trials in the development of airborne radar.

COURTESY PHILIP JARRETT

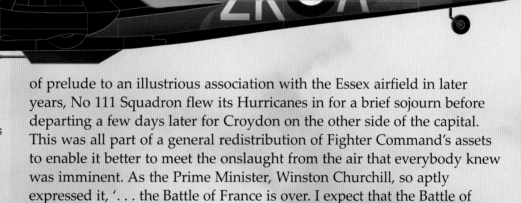

Below: A profile of L6676, another Blenheim IF on the strength of No 25 Squadron at North Weald.

Below: Two-bladed Hurricane Is of No 111 Squadron, seen here at RAF Northolt in a publicity photograph showing the pilots eager to get airborne. A brief stay at North Weald in June 1940 heralded a longer period of residence for the Squadron the following year—and more permanent settlement in the 1950s.

of prelude to an illustrious association with the Essex airfield in later years, No 111 Squadron flew its Hurricanes in for a brief sojourn before departing a few days later for Croydon on the other side of the capital. This was all part of a general redistribution of Fighter Command's assets to enable it better to meet the onslaught from the air that everybody knew was imminent. As the Prime Minister, Winston Churchill, so aptly expressed it, '. . . the Battle of France is over. I expect that the Battle of Britain is about to begin.'

Begin it most certainly did, and over the next few months the RAF squadrons at North Weald found themselves in the thick of the aerial conflict that would determine the fate of the nation. Although the

45

Left: Pilots of No 249 Squadron pose with their Hurricane Mk Is at North Weald—a photograph taken in autumn 1940, shortly after the Battle of Britain.
Below: The cockpit of a Hurricane, showing the main instrument panel and compass below, the control stick, and the gun firing button at the top left of the hand grip.

COURTESY NWAM

Luftwaffe had been making raids on eastern and southern England since the spring of 1940, the battle really started in the middle of July, with heavy raids on the coastal towns. The picture soon changed, however, when fighter airfields such as North Weald, Biggin Hill, Hornchurch and Tangmere began to come under attack. On 24 August North Weald suffered a large raid by German bombers; it is recorded that over 200 bombs fell on the airfield, resulting in serious damage. Married quarters allocated to both officers and airmen were struck and nine members of the Essex Regiment were killed when their shelter received a direct hit. Ten other air force personnel were injured in the raid. Almost before the Station could recover, the Germans returned on 31 August to strike again. Despite No 56 Squadron launching some twelve Hurricanes to meet the enemy, the reported 200 raiders divided into smaller groups, one of which headed for North Weald. It was the practice for the Luftwaffe to escort its bomber formations with the highly potent Messerschmitt Bf 109 single-engine and Bf 110 twin-engine fighters, and this day was no exception. Totally outnumbered, the Hurricanes lost four aircraft early in the engagement. In all, as a result of these German forays, No 56 had lost eleven aircraft, and on 1 September the Squadron was removed to Boscombe Down for rest and re-equipment. No 151 Squadron had suffered too, and on 29 August was transferred to nearby Stapleford Tawney aerodrome, although they stayed for a few days only before being relocated to RAF Digby. The Squadron had lost two pilots and six Hurricanes, and their CO Donaldson departed for pastures new.

The Battle of Britain was still being fought tenaciously in the skies over south-east England, and even though Nos 56 Squadron needed to retire temporarily from the fray there was no let up in activity for North Weald. Their place was immediately taken by No 249 Squadron, whose person-nel, led by Squadron Leader J. Grandy and already primed for combat

No 249 Squadron
Motto
Pugnis et Calcibus
('With Fists and Heels')
Equipment
Hawker Hurricane Mk I (1940),
Hawker Hurricane Mk IIA/IIB
(1941)

Above: The Officers' Mess at North Weald was situated off the aerodrome proper, in the domestic site to the south, across the main Epping–Ongar road. It exists today, refurb-ished, as Norway House.

No 46 Squadron

Motto
We Rise to Conquer

Equipment
Hawker Hurricane Mk I (1940)

following spells at Church Fenton and Boscombe Down, flew in on 1 September to take over No 56's aircraft. At Stapleford Tawney, No 46 Squadron arrived on the same day, 1 September, for a two-month stay flying Hurricanes before transferring briefly to North Weald and then to Digby. This squadron had recently been embarked on the aircraft carrier HMS *Glorious* for operations over Norway, its pilots having successfully undertaken the hazardous task of landing on board without the benefit of arrester hooks, although, sadly, eight of its pilots and all its aircraft had been lost on 9 June while being evacuated when the carrier was sunk.

In addition to the front-line fighter squadrons, North Weald was home from time to time for a number of smaller units, several of them of a secretive nature and usually dispersed about the airfield, out of sight as far as possible from prying eyes. During 1940, for example, and at the special request of Prime Minister Churchill, Westland Lysanders were located in the north-east corner, their short take-off and landing capability enabling them to fly out and collect special operatives to and from enemy-held territory. Twin-engined Armstrong Whitworth Whitley bombers—No 419 Flight—are also known to have been stationed at North Weald during the summer of that year, although the intensity of the German attacks forced a move to Stapleford Tawney. The Whitleys were also tasked with the delivery of special operatives behind enemy lines, but it was quickly appreciated that Stapleford's runways were incapable of handling these heavy aircraft and the unit moved to Stradishall in October 1940.

'Fifty-plus Bandits Approaching'

From the Diary of Pilot Officer Tom Neil, pilot, No 249 Squadron

We landed, taxied in quickly and the bowsers lumbered forward to hook up and began refuelling. My airscrew tottered to a standstill. Crew members on the wing roots.

'Everything all right, Sir?' New faces, but eager and smiling.

'Fine'.

'Turn round quickly!' was the urgent instruction. We needed no persuading. My own aircraft was full but some of the others weren't when the air-raid siren began its banshee wail and our second scramble order came. 'Patrol base' this time. Crikey! That didn't sound so good.

I raced across the grass to my position on John Grandy's right. Then, full throttle, 3,000 revs and off again. Wheels up – I didn't even look. The masts drifted past. Climbing like hell. The squadron strung out. Cutting corners and catching up. Climb! Climb! Hell's bells! We couldn't climb any faster. My throttle lever was at full stretch. Being up front, I was all right, but think of the poor blighters behind!

From Sector: 'Fifty-plus bandits [enemy aircraft] approaching from the south-east. Angels 17 [17,000 feet]'.

We clawed our way up, my engine raging. Through 7,000 feet . . .10,000 feet . . .up to 12,000, flying roughly east.

Then above and at eleven o'clock—ack-ack fire! Faint, growing smudges . . . pecking . . . more ack-ack . . . blossoming—a growling cluster of it. Everything was in slow motion. Then, aircraft in the middle of the puffs. Huns! Oh God! Masses of them! Tally-ho! My eyes glued to them. Fascinated . . . growing closer . . . clearer now . . . large ones in front and in the middle. Others like flies, stepped up and behind. Thousands, it seemed—and there were only twelve of us!

We were below and to the south. The River Blackwater was in the background and they were heading due west. We turned slowly to the left, climbing hard still. I could see them properly now. The bombers were Dornier 17s, the fighters were Me 110s, forging steadily ahead. Streak through the flowering puffs of ack-ack, taking no notice, oblivious.

The CO said in a tense voice, 'Steady, Ganer [call-sign for No 249] Squadron'.

I was aware that I was the outside of the aircraft on the right of the formation, looking up to my left towards the bombers and above and to the right of the Messerschmitts.

The 110's were close now—very close. I could see them clearly—some sort of coloured markings on the nearest aircraft. I was going to pass right underneath! If they choose to come down, we are finished. Closer . . . turning to the left still and going hard, but I couldn't hit any of the any of the bombers from here! They were the important ones—to heck with the fighters! Right underneath now, I could reach up and touch them. Why on earth weren't they coming down? My head bent right back. One Me 110 suspended above me—I could feel its airscrews rotating.

Then, wings flashing, my leader turning on its back. Other aircraft were diving . . . a moment of utter surprise and panic . . . mustn't be left! I tumbled after them in pursuit. What was happening? Were we being attacked? I kept screwing my head around but could see nothing. My Hurricane dropped like a stone, dust rising from around my feet, my head pressed against the roof of the cockpit, other aircraft on my left. Diving like hell, rolling out. Hurricanes! I joined them—John Grandy's aircraft. But I hadn't fired! I hadn't had time to fire!

The RT and a voice from below - high pitched with excitement but controlled. 'We've been hit, Ganer Squadron!'

But we are all right. I look over the side. To my surprise, we are directly above North Weald and, far below, the whole airfield is hidden beneath a huge, spreading, grey-brown pall of smoke and dust. They'd bombed us! The airfield—the blighters had bombed our airfield! It never occurred to me that we might not be able to land on it.

I looked up. Far above, aircraft were turning away northwards. Were they the bombers? I couldn't see. Join up! I looked about. I was in a formation of sorts. More Hurricanes were surging into position . . . urgently . . . rocking

Above: Tom Neil (far right) with members of the No 249 Squadron ground crew. The Hurricane carries the personal marking 'Wynne'..

. . . bouncing with tilting wings. We flew around; the sky was suddenly clear—magically. Then the 'pancake' instruction. We began to let down – but I hadn't fired—not a single bullet. I turned my gun button to 'Safe'.

We flew in from the direction of the Marconi masts, in rough sections of three, and touched down across the concrete, weaving gently between the bomb-holes. Within twenty minutes, all twelve Hurricanes had been refuelled and were ready for take-off. Two hangars had been hit, we were told. We could see the smoke but had not the time to go over to the far side of the airfield—nor, indeed, did I particularly want to.

Tom Neil—now Wing Commander Tom Neil DFC* AFC—mentions two other items in his writings worthy of note. Of Station Commander Beamish, he says: 'Earlier, I had met the Station Commander— a smiling, affable man of about 38. I immediately sensed that if you flew and pulled your weight— fine! If you didn't—curtains! He flew one of our Hurricanes wearing the letter 'B', the Squadron holding one aircraft above establishment for the purpose.'

The night of the North Weald raid, two German aircraft were shot down by Pilot Officer Herrick of No 25 Squadron in a Blenheim. Neil comments: 'In my opinion, anyone brave enough to take off in a fighter Blenheim deserves a gong—and here he is shooting down two Huns within minutes!'

Some feeling for the effects on the ground of the raid can be gained from the history of Epping Fire Brigade:

'On Tuesday the Aerodrome was bombed again, this time mid-morning [sic]. Epping Urban of course attended but there was not much chance of liaison, as just about everything had been hit and there was much to do . . .

'Eventually we made contact with Harlow Brigade, who entered the 'drome from the far side and had a serious fire to contend with in a hangar there. They were furious, for when they arrived the fire had only just reached a Blenheim bomber in the hangar, so had there been anyone about who could have released the brake they could have towed it clear. But not a soul was to be seen! The result was that, by the time they had got a line run out and water on, the plane was a total loss'

Below: The bombed-out hangar with the wreckage of a Blenheim.

"LET US GO FORWARD TOGETHER"

Right: Blake Hall, a Grade II* listed stately home dating back to the seventeenth century, The south wing (to the right in this photograph) was refurbished during the war to serve as the Operations Room for Sector E, No 11 Group, directing RAF air activity for North Weald and its associated airfields.

Another German raid on North Weald came on 3 September. No 249 Squadron had just landed when a 'scramble' was called. Most of the aircraft were still in the process of re-arming and refuelling, but they took off all the same. With the advantage of altitude, however, the Luftwaffe bombers were releasing their deadly loads before the Hurricanes could engage them. Once more the airfield suffered severe damage, with hangars and the MT yard being hit and set ablaze. Aircraft, living quarters, the Operations Room and other station buildings had been destroyed, leaving five people dead and 39 injured. To add to the tragedy, three Blenheims from No 25 Squadron, L1409, L1512 and L8586, were fired on and damaged by No 46 Squadron Hurricanes over Greensted, near Ongar, in a 'friendly fire' incident, killing the pilot of the one aircraft that was actually shot down though, fortunately, sparing the remaining five crewmen. Thereafter a lull in attacks on the airfield enabled repairs to be carried out, and the decision was now made to move the Station

COURTESY NWAM

Left, upper: Just as hard-pressed as the pilots during the fateful months of 1940 were the support personnel—ground crews, maintenance men and administrative staff. Everything possible was done to ensure that the maximum number of aircraft were available for combat at all times. Here in a hangar at North Weald a Hurricane of No 151 Squadron is undergoing repair, the peeled-off fabric revealing something of the aircraft's wooden rear fuselage framing.

Left, lower: A wingless No 249 Squadron Hurricane, P3154, on a Queen Mary low-loader and ready for transport to a maintenance unit for major repair. The aircraft's individual identity letter, forward of the (non-standard) fuselage roundel, seems to have been obliterated.

COURTESY NWAM

Above: Detail view of the main hangar area, with the Officer's Mess at top right, across the road, late 1940.

Headquarters, followed later by the Operations Room, off the aerodrome to Blake Hall, a historic stately home in Bobbingworth, some four miles to the east.

The air battle grew in intensity as the month of September unfolded, the North Weald squadrons losing eleven Hurricanes in the space of five days. Gradually, however, the emphasis of the Luftwaffe's onslaught began to switch from raids on Fighter Command's assets to attacks on the City of London, where the docks and industrial complexes received particular attention from the bomb-laden Dorniers and Heinkels. Here again, echoing the heroic exploits of North Weald's pioneer fighter pilots twenty-four years before, the men and machines of North Weald were tasked with the defence of the capital.

Following the departure of Nos 56 and 151 Squadrons, during September and early October No 249 Squadron was the sole Hurricane-equipped unit at the airfield, although of course the Blenheims of No 25 were still very active. By the end of September the latter unit had begun to receive new equipment in the form of the Bristol Beaufighter, having, the previous July, taken on strength a couple of single-seat Westland

"NEVER WAS SO MUCH OWED BY SO MANY TO SO FEW" *THE PRIME MINISTER*

The Chianti Raiders

The Author

Often overlooked is the fact that the United Kingdom was attacked from the air during World War II not only by the Luftwaffe but also by the Regia Aeronautica (Italian Air Force), which raided the south-east of the mainland on more than one occasion. The attackers were known colloquially as the Chianti Raiders, and one such incursion in the skies over North Weald took place on

11 November 1940, shortly after the Battle of Britain, mounted by aircraft flying from airfields at Chièvres and Ursel in Belgium.

In response to this attack, No 249 Squadron, led by Beamish, were airborne over the Thames Estuary, although several pilots of the Squadron failed to reach their rendezvous as a result of bad weather. Doug Stokes, in his biography of Beamish (*Wings Aflame*, 1985), relates the story:

'Possibly because of the weather, but more likely because he wanted some freelance action, Beamish headed out east on his own, flying through mist and cloud towards where the Italians were reported by the North Weald controller. Picking up the coastline through the murk east of Harwich he joined the mêlée. Beamish closed to 100 yards on the two [Fiat] C.R.42s and raked them with three-second bursts, drawing smoke from the second biplane which half-rolled into a vertical dive in the haze over the sea. Looking to Beamish . . . he went straight in some 20–30 miles east of Southwold . . . [Beamish] returned to North Weald to claim the C.R.42 as probably destroyed.'

Left: A C.R.42 fighter brought down while escorting a raid by Italian bombers over south-east England

COURTESY NWAM

No 257 Squadron

Motto
Thay Myay Gyee Shin Shwe Hti
('Death or Glory')

Equipment
Hawker Hurricane Mk I (1940)

Whirlwind twin-engine, cannon-armed fighters in order to evaluate their suitability for as replacements for the faithful Blenheims—although their effectiveness as night fighters would surely have been compromised by the absence of any radar equipment. It was during the course of receiving the Beaufighter that No 25 Squadron was removed from North Weald and relocated at Debden a few miles to the north near the border with Cambridgeshire. On the day they departed, 8 October, the vacancy was filled by another Hurricane squadron, No 257, transferred from Martlesham Heath and led by one of the most renowned fighter aces of World War II—Squadron Leader R. R. S. Stanford-Tuck.

Royal Air Force losses continued to be high during this period—and not merely in the air. Any illusion of 'safety' within the airfields once the Germans had changed tactics and turned their attention to London was cruelly dispelled on 29 October when bomb-toting Messerschmitt 109s of LG.2 hit North Weald once again, catching the two Hurricane squadrons on the ground and costing the lives of a further six people, including a civilian.

The attack of 29 October proved to be the last enemy air raid on North Weald in the Battle of Britain. During that period—10 July to 31 October—forty-one North Weald aircrew had been killed along with seventeen groundcrew. Nevertheless, although it had suffered greatly as a result of the attacks, the airfield had managed to remain operational during daylight hours throughout this critical period.

Right: Hurricane I of No 257 Squadron, as flown by Squadron Leader Bob Stanford-Tuck while he was stationed at North Weald in autumn of 1940. The aircraft is decorated with 'kill' markings and a jovial caricature of Churchill.

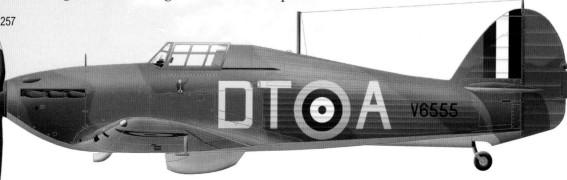

TURNING THE TIDE

AS the winter of 1940/41 closed in, the tempo of flying operations began to dwindle, and RAF Fighter Command took the opportunity to regroup and prepare for the next phase of the conflict. No 257 Squadron's brief stay at North Weald came to an close on 8 October when the its aircraft and personnel returned to Martlesham Heath. No 46 Squadron departed on 14 December, and three days later some old friends were welcomed back to the airfield when No 56 Squadron

Eagles over Essex

The Author

As Britain came under ever more sustained attack during the first year of the war, countries from the British Empire began to offer weapons and manpower to help defend the mother country. Aircrews from European nations that had suffered under the advance of the Third Reich, for example Poland, also arrived in Britain and pitched in to assist in the repulse of the common foe. Less generally appreciated is the fact that US personnel also volunteered.

Very strict laws in the United States governed the supply of arms to other countries, and these applied to personnel also. It was against Federal Law for US citizens to join armed forces of other nations, and to do so would lose them their American citizenship. Even so, many found ways to circumvent these statutes and cross the Atlantic to fight for the British cause.

Back in 1939, Colonel Charles Sweeney, an American mercenary financier, had tried to raise troops to fight in the Russo-Finnish War but following the German invasions in Europe he had turned his attention to France. None of his recruits actually got to France, but many did find their way to England. Meanwhile Sweeney's nephew

was trying to get US pilots to join the Royal Air Force, having first encouraged Americans living in England to join the Home Guard units. Buoyed by his success, he then approached the Air Ministry with the idea of creating 'American' squadrons in the RAF—a scheme which met with enthusiasm and the founding of the so-called 'Eagle Squadrons', Nos 71, 121 and 133, all under the leadership of RAF officers. Over fifty pilots had by various means managed to arrive covertly in the United Kingdom, many by way of Canada. The organisation of these transfers was in the hands of World War I pilot Air Vice-Marshal Billy Bishop VC through what was known as the Clayton Knight Committee, a quite illegal organisation. In due course the Committee succeeded in recruiting over 7,000 US and Canadian people for the RAF, and it continued its campaign until the United States officially entered the war as a combatant nation in December 1941.

Below: A Hurricane Mk I from No 71 Squadron running its engine as another passes overhead. By the time the unit flew into North Weald, it had taken delivery of Mk IIBs—although it would soon relinquish these in favour of Spitfires.

COURTESY PHILIP JARRETT

No 71 (Eagle) Squadron

Motto
First from the Eyries

Equipment
Hawker Hurricane Mk IIB (1941), Supermarine Spitfire Mk IIA (1941), Supermarine Spitfire Mk VB (1941)

No 121 (Eagle) Squadron

Motto
For Liberty

Equipment
Supermarine Spitfire Mk VB (1941–1942)

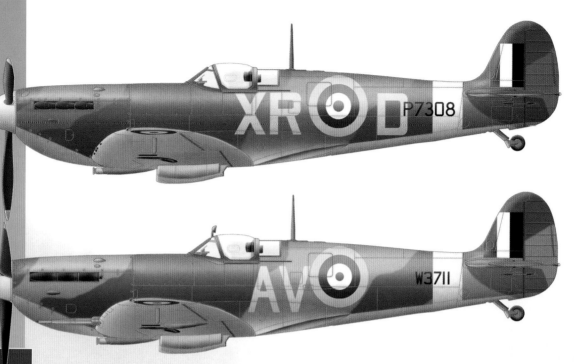

Right, upper: A profile of a Spitfire Mk IIA of No 71 (Eagle) Squadron. The Sky-painted band around the rear fuselage helped identify friendly aircraft.

Right, lower: A profile of a No 121 Squadron Spitfire Mk VB showing the new Fighter Command colour scheme—Ocean Grey and Dark Green camouflage, with Medium Sea Grey undersurfaces.

SUPERMARINE SPITFIRE Mk IIA
Type: Fighter
Engine: One 1,150hp Rolls-Royce Merlin XII inline
Length: 29ft 11in (9.12m)
Wing span: 36ft 10in (11.23m)
Speed: 357mph (575kph) max.
Range: 500 miles (805km) max.
Service ceiling: 37,200ft (12,200m)
Armament: Eight 0.303in Browning machine guns
Crew: Pilot only

COURTESY NWAM

Above : Scrawled messages and a dilapidated bicycle mark the No 71 Squadron Headquarters at North Weald, 1941.

returned with its Hurricanes, having spent the past three months in the West Country.

By this time Hawker's development team had finished work on an upgrade for the Hurricane from Mk I to Mk II, which incorporated a more powerful Merlin engine and a revised wing which, in due course, would be able to carry twelve rather than eight machine guns or, optionally, four 20mm Hispano cannon. The Mk II began to enter service in the autumn of 1940, and No 56 Squadron started to receive replacement aircraft in February 1941.

The first of the Eagle Squadrons was the re-formed No 71 Squadron, a fighter unit equipped with Hurricane Is, initially based at Kirton-in-Lindsey and then, on being declared operational, at Martlesham Heath. In June 1941, the unit moved to North Weald as one half of the North Weald Wing, now equipped with Mk IIs. Tasked with offensive missions over Europe, the Squadron flew sweeps, bomber escorts and convoy patrols, working some distance away from base as demonstrated by Squadron's first 'kill' —the destruction over Lille of an Me 109 on 21 July by Pilot Officer Dunn.

In August 1941 came a change in equipment when Spitfire Mk IIAs were taken on to inventory. Night training and a rumoured move overseas, together with a relative lack of success in the air had led to some difficulties with morale within the Squadron, but success came when the summer skies returned and the 'kill' tally went up. The Spitfire IIAs were supplanted by more potent Mk VBs towards the end of the year, and the unit said farewell to North Weald in December 1941 and returned to Martlesham Heath.

The second of the Eagle Squadrons to see service at North Weald was No 121, re-formed at Kirton-in-Lindsey in May 1941 and transferring to the Essex airfield in December, its equipment also by this time Spitfire VBs. No 121's routine of offensive attacks over the near-Continent was

interrupted in February when the squadron was involved in the notoriously unsuccessful attempt to prevent the German battlecruisers *Gneisenau* and *Scharnhorst* and the heavy cruiser *Prinz Eugen* dashing for their home ports through the English Channel. Success came to No 121 Squadron's Pilot Officer Mooney, however, with the destruction of the first of many Focke-Wulf FW 190s. Forays over France started to become the norm for the unit from the spring of 1942.

Naturally enough, following the Japanese attack on Pearl Harbor on 7 December 1941 and the entry of the United States into the war, most of the Americans wished to join their own forces and, as a result, the three Eagle Squadrons were eventually, on 29 September 1942, transferred to the US Army Air Forces, becoming collectively the 4th Fighter Group. The USAAF formed three fighter squadrons in the 4th FG, Nos 334, 335 and 336, which all continued to fly Spitfires until the arrival of replacement P-47 Thunderbolts from the United States.

So ended North Weald's first experience of overseas participation in its war—an experience felt by the military and civilians alike. The bravery shown and sacrifice made by these young Americans in the defence of our nation, much of their flying taking place long before their mother country was officially drawn into the conflict, should not be forgotten. No 71 Squadron scored 41 aerial victories and No 121 scored 18, and 82 of these men lost their lives. In 1944, a general pardon was granted to all US personnel who had crossed the Atlantic to serve with the RAF.

Just as the first of the North Weald's Eagle Squadrons was preparing to take up residence at the airfield, on 21 May 1941 No 249 Squadron's Hurricanes departed for the balmy climes of the Mediterranean in order to help defend the strategically vital island of Malta. Their place was taken the next day by No 242 Squadron, flying Hurricane IIBs and principally Canadian-manned—and until March 1941 commanded by Squadron Leader Douglas Bader, champion of the RAF's not wholly successful 'Big Wing' tactics. No 242 had for the previous six weeks been operating out of Stapleford Tawney. No 242 did not remain at North Weald for long, however, being ordered to Manston in Kent in mid-July although they would return briefly, re-equipped with Spitfire Vs, a year later.

The departure of No 56 Squadron and arrival of No 71 in June was a prelude to further reshuffling when, on 20 July, No 111 Squadron flew in for a five-month stay and, on 18 August, No 222 Squadron touched down. The two newcomers were Spitfire units, and with No 71 by this time also completing their conversion to the Supermarine fighter—the three units now making up the North Weald Wing—the sight of a Hurricane in the skies over West Essex was beginning to become an unusual occurrence.

One interesting aspect of No 111's 1941 deployment to North Weald is the evaluation of their Spitfires as prospective night fighters, to counter

Above: A profile showing a Hurricane Mk IIB of No 242 Squadron. The Hurricane Mk II improved upon the early Battle of Britain-era aircraft in having a more powerful, supercharged Merlin engine and an upgraded armament. The IIB, for example, was fitted with twelve instead of eight machine guns.

No 242 Squadron

Motto
Toujours Prêt
('Always Ready')

Equipment
Hawker Hurricane Mk IIB
(1941)

No 222 Squadron

Motto
Pambili Bo
('Go Straight Ahead')

Equipment
Supermarine Spitfire Mk IIA/IIB
(1941), Supermarine Spitfire
Mk VB (1941–1942)

Right: A Spitfire Mk VB of No 222 Squadron. By this time yellow-painted wing leading edges had been introduced on RAF fighters—another aid to recognition in the air, particularly to a pilot who was being followed.

Right: An experimental Spitfire Mk VB night fighter of No 111 Squadron. The capabilities of these aircraft were limited, one reason being their inability to carry any radar equipment.

Below; Colour photographs of World War II RAF aircraft are not plentiful, but this is one of an official series taken of No 222 Squadron's Spitfire VBs at North Weald in May 1942 (or so the caption says—although the crops appear decidedly ripe for that time of year!). Interestingly, the aircraft is being flown by Richard Milne, whom we met earlier while flying Hurricanes on No 151 Squadron.

any repeat of the Blitz that the Germans might have had in mind. To this end, a number of their aircraft were finished with black paintwork overall. Interception of enemy bombers by single-seat aircraft was an extremely difficult task, however, and the trials, which began late in 1941, just as the Squadron was preparing to leave for Debden, were later abandoned.

No 222 Squadron, equipped with Spitfire VBs, was tasked mainly with sweeps over France, bomber escort and acting as what we would today refer to as an 'aggressor' squadron to support the Eagles' training. They also flew with No 121 Squadron during the 'Channel Dash' by German heavy warships referred to earlier.

No 222 remained at North Weald for well over a year, but with the movement of units to and from the heart of the battle in Europe, very many other squadrons passed through the airfield at this hectic time, some of them staying for a matter of days only.

IMPERIAL WAR MUSEUM

The departure of No 71 Squadron in December 1941 was complemented by the arrival not only of the second Eagle Squadron, No 121 (see above), but also No 403. The former had arrived on the 16th and the latter, a unit manned exclusively by Canadian personnel, flew in eight days later, equipped with Spitfire Mk VBs. The Canadians remained until 2 May 1942 and were engaged primarily in offensive sweeps over northern France and the Low Countries. A second RCAF unit, No 412 (all Canadian squadrons were by this time numbered in the '400' series), stopped over at North Weald for a couple of weeks the following month.

It was not Britain's highly valued Commonwealth allies that were to have the greatest impact on North Weald during the latter years of the

Above: Another in the series of official photographs of No 222 Squadron at North Weald, this doubtless posed photograph—seemingly taken at a different time of the year—shows plenty of activity surrounding one of the Squadron's Spitfires as it is 'turned around' between sorties. Below: Profiles showing Spitfire VBs of No 403 (upper) and 412 (lower) Squadrons, the first two Canadian units to be based at North Weald.

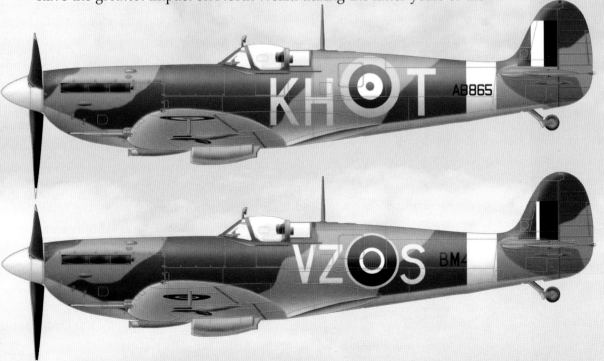

Right: A Spitfire Mk VA in the markings of No 332 Squadron in June 1942.

No 403 Squadron

Motto
Stalk and Strike

Equipment
Supermarine Spitfire Mk VB
(1941–1942)

No 412 Squadron

Motto
Promptus ad Vindictum
('Swift to Avenge')

Equipment
Supermarine Spitfire Mk VB
(1942)

Right: A No 331 Squadron Spitfire Mk VB. The application of the recognition band around the rear fuselage often obscured the serial number.

war, neither did the aerodrome, like so many RAF airfields, host scores of US aircraft: improbable though it must have seemed at the time, North Weald and its environs were to forge strong and lasting bonds, and friendships that endure to this day, with one of our northernmost neighbours—Norway.

Limited liaison between North Weald and the Norwegians had taken place during the Zeppelin campaign in World War I when, concerned about the possible effect that the airships could have if used against their own country, the government of Norway requested a transfer of information between the British and Norwegian authorities. To assist in this endeavour, a Norwegian officer (known, for security reasons, as 'Captain Grant') was seconded to No 39 (HD) Squadron to fly alongside aircrew in their B.E.12s.

In 1940, despite a heroic defence by its countrymen, supported by the British and French, Norway fell to the Germans in the late spring. As happened in several occupied European countries, many pilots managed to escape to Britain and were able to join the RAF and continue the fight. Initially formed at Catterick, two Norwegian-manned squadrons, Nos 331 and 332, moved to North Weald in, respectively, May and June 1942 following a period in the Orkneys to help defend Scapa Flow. They were thus founder units of the Royal Norwegian Air Force.

While most Royal Air Force fighter units were regularly redeployed around the country during the conflict, the Norwegians remained at North Weald until the requirements of D-Day obliged them to move. The terms of the agreement between Britain and Norway meant that the Norwegians paid to be equipped initially (their aircraft were leased from the RAF), paid an annual fee, paid for the repair and maintenance of such equipment in first class condition at all times, and covered the costs of losses, repairs, parts, servicing, fuel, weapons, ammunition, billeting, transport and messing. It was deemed easier to maintain the accounts if the whole system stayed in one place rather than splitting the deployment across several airfields. The squadrons were funded by money raised from Norway's merchant marine, and the men were paid separately from RAF personnel and enjoyed a different structure of ranking.

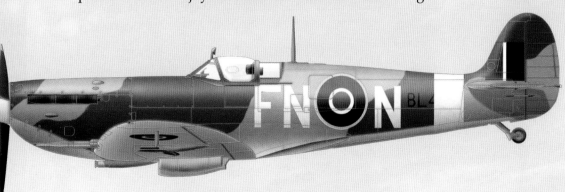

The Dieppe Raid

The Author

One of the Allied disasters of World War II, the so-called Dieppe Raid was an attempt to occupy a port in enemy-held Europe, so forming a bridge-head, in order to gain intelligence from prisoners, destroy coastal defences and evaluate the German responses to such a venture. Utilising more than seventy squadrons of aircraft, mostly Spitfires, for the expedition, the Allies appeared to have the advantage but would be fighting at the extent of their range, with, in the case of the covering aircraft, very few minutes over target.

The original operation, code-named 'Rutter', was scheduled to take place between 4 and 8 July 1942 but was cancelled at the last moment owing to inclement weather and a suspicion that the Germans had got wind of the plan. It was, however, resurrected the next month as Operation 'Jubilee' and got under way in the evening of 18 August. The venture was a total failure and a retreat was in place by 0940 hours the following day at the cost of some 4,000 servicemen, Canadian and

British, captured, killed or wounded. A total of 106 aircraft were lost by the Allies against 44 German, the Spitfire Vs finding themselves outclassed by the superior FW 190s. Both Nos 331 and 332 Squadrons were involved in the battle, the former scoring three FW 190 'kills' and four damaged, at a cost of two Spitfires; No 332 downed three FW 190s and five Do 217s for the loss of four fighters. One of the raid's outcomes was the setting up of the Second Tactical Air Force.

Below: BM579, a No 331 Squadron Spitfire VB, wearing special recognition markings adopted for Operation 'Rutter'.

COURTESY NWAM

No 331 (Norwegian) Squadron

Motto
For Norge
('For Norway')

Equipment
Supermarine Spitfire Mk VB (1942), Supermarine Spitfire Mk IX (1942–1944)

Equipped with Spitfire Vs, the Norwegians found themselves thrown instantly into the fray. No 331, with Mk VBs, scored one 'probable' and one damaged on 19 May while on only its second sortie, and on the 31st gained its first victory against an Me 109. Joining 331 on 19 June with, initially, Spitfire Mk VAs, No 332 joined the routing of regular raids across the Channel. Its first victories also came on 31 July: an FW 190 and an Me 109 were shot down, albeit at the high cost of four of the Squadron's own aircraft.

After a summer of raids across the Channel, including the Dieppe Raid, the winter months brought about the usual easing of flying operations, allowing both No 331 and No 332 to get used to their new Spitfire Mk IX, which, with a bigger engine and a more powerful armament than its predecessors, had been brought into service as a response to the Germans' impressive FW 190. The year 1943 was, for the most part, devoted to the provision of fighter escort for the ever increasing number of Allied bomber raids into Europe, and the emphasis in early 1944 switched to the pending invasion of the Continent. Now part of the fully integrated Second Tactical Air Force, the squadrons had to learn new tactics for this and spent many flying hours perfecting the art of dive-bombing.

In late March 1944, just prior to D-Day, the two squadrons of the Norwegian Wing left North Weald for Bognor, thereby ending their service in Essex. The final mission of World War II involving the Wing

No 332 (Norwegian) Squadron

Motto
Samhold i Strid
('Together in Battle')

Equipment
Supermarine Spitfire Mk VB (1942), Supermarine Spitfire Mk IX (1942–1944)

Below: A profile of the specially marked Spitfire VB depicted in the photograph above.

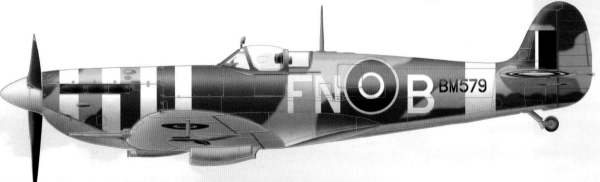

BM579

SUPERMARINE SPITFIRE Mk VB
Type: Fighter
Engine: One 1,440hp Rolls-Royce Merlin 45, 46, 50 or 50A
Length: 29ft 11in (9.12m)
Wing span: 36ft 10in (11.23m)
Weight: 6,650lb (3,020kg) loaded
Speed: 374mph (600kph) maximum
Range: 470 miles (760km)
Armament: Two 20mm cannon and four 0.303in Browning machine guns
Crew: Pilot only

Right: Three of North Weald's Norwegian pilots discuss tactics. The Spitfire VB in the background carries the personal name 'Litago'.

Above: A Norwegian pilot in the cockpit of his Spitfire, which shows 'kill' markings beneath the windshield.
Below; Spitfire VBs of No 332 Squadron await the next sortie at North Weald as two others roar overhead at ultra low level.

took place on 21 April 1945 when its aircraft escorted a bombing raid on Oldenburg carried by USAAF B-25 Mitchells. Leaving their mounts at the Dutch base of Twente, the crews returned to North Weald one more time to collect brand new Spitfire Mk IXEs and head home. The tally of the Wing had been, to say the least, remarkable—180½ 'kills', 25½ 'probables' and 132 enemy aircraft damaged, in addition to which it was credited with the destruction of 381 road vehicles, 62 locomotives, 70 railway wagons, thirteen tanks and 134 assorted enemy vehicles. The cost—and it must never be forgotten that the Norwegian personnel were defending our country as their own—was 36 pilots killed while flying from North Weald, as well as 36 lost during the German occupation of Norway and eleven taken prisoner. In his appraisal of their contribution to the Dieppe Raid, for example, Station CO Wing Commander David Scott-Malden famously remarked that the Norwegians formed the best aerial fighting unit of the war.

The effect of the Norwegians' sojourn at North Weald cannot be underestimated. Officers and aircrew alike socialised in nearby Epping in their

COURTESY NWAM

COURTESY NWAM

No 124 Squadron

Motto
Danger is our Opportunity

Equipment
Supermarine Spitfire Mk VI
(1942), Supermarine Spitfire
Mk VII (1943)

Left: By summer 1943 both No
331 and No 332 Squadrons had
exchanged their Spitfire Mk Vs
for more powerful Mk IXs,
better to counter the more
advanced German fighters then
coming into service. Speeds of
over 400mph could now be
routinely achieved. The upper
photograph shows a No 332
Squadron Mk IX at dispersal
and the lower photograph illustrates gun-cleaning in progress.

No 486 Squadron

Motto
Hiwa Hau Maka
('Beware of the Wild Winds')

Equipment
Hawker Typhoon Mk IB (1942)

rest hours, and many relationships flourished. Before the Wing returned to Norway at the end of hostilities, marriages and families had grown out of the time spent here, and when the day came for the airmen to return to Norway, large numbers of the local villagers turned out to bid them farewell. In later years, after the airfield closed for RAF operations, the Officers' Mess across the main Epping–Ongar road was converted into residential accommodation for the homeless and called Norway House, in honour of the young Norwegians who frequented it.

In 1952, Princess Astrid of Norway unveiled a commemorative stone at the entrance to what is now the North Weald Airfield Museum, thanking the RAF and the people of North Weald for the support that they gave to their Norwegian neighbours during these dark days. Some sixty years later, an annual memorial service is still held, more often than not attended by a high-ranking Norwegian official.

The two Norwegian squadrons were the principal occupants of North Weald aerodrome during their stay from May 1942 to June 1944, but there were plenty of other squadrons to be seen from time to time, bringing with them new shapes in the sky. After about a year in residence, other than a six-week deployment to Manston, No 222 Squadron departed on 1 August 1942, and the following month witnessed a brief visit by New

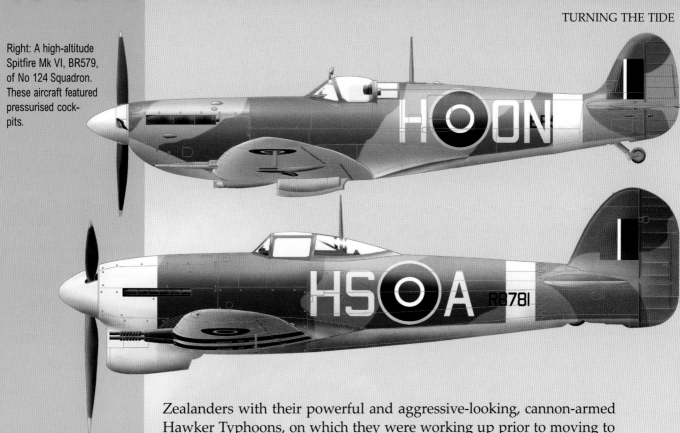

Right: A high-altitude Spitfire Mk VI, BR579, of No 124 Squadron. These aircraft featured pressurised cockpits.

Above: A profile of a Hawker Typhoon of No 486 Squadron, illustrating early recognition markings in the form of a white forward fuselage (soon abandoned) and black and white underwing stripes (retained).

Zealanders with their powerful and aggressive-looking, cannon-armed Hawker Typhoons, on which they were working up prior to moving to their main base, RAF Tangmere, for operations over northern France. They remained at North Weald for a fortnight. In November, unusual aircraft in the form of high-altitude Spitfire Mk VIs were seen when No 124 Squadron arrived, staying for a month but returning briefly the following March with Mk VIIs in the same rôle. The aircraft were distinguishable chiefly by their extended, pointed wing tips, offering the pilots a few extra hundreds of feet in an effort to counter high-flying German reconnaissance aircraft.

The year 1943 saw no further newcomers until November, when two RAF squadrons of North American Mustangs flew in. These aircraft, which were to become the backbone of the USAAF's fighter escort

HAWKER TYPHOON Mk IB
Type: Ground-attack fighter
Engine: One 2,180hp Napier Sabre IIA
Length: 31ft 11in (9.73m)
Wing span: 41ft 7in (12.67m)
Weight: 13,250lb (6,000kg) loaded
Speed: 412mph (660kph) maximum
Range: 510 miles (820km)
Armament: Four 20mm cannon and two 1,000lb (450kg) bombs
Crew: Pilot only

Right: The airfield in August 1942, looking south-west; the main hangars are at top left. Twenty or so Spitfires of the North Weald Wing are visible. Fake 'rivers' and a 'pond' have been painted along the runways, and fake 'hedgerows' are seen in the centre of the photograph.

COURTESY NWAM

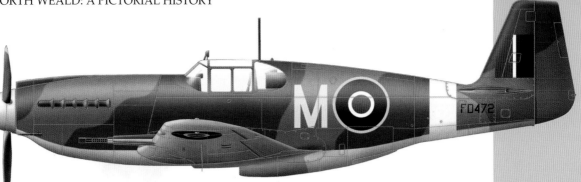

inventory once their Allison engines had been replaced by Rolls-Royce Merlins to enable them to operate effectively at medium and high altitudes, were employed principally in the low-altitude fighter-reconnaissance rôle, and they ranged over the English Channel and northern France, attacking enemy shipping and targets of opportunity and gathering intelligence. Flying these aircraft, No 4 Squadron, on Mk Is, was at North Weald from 15 to 30 November 1943 before moving a few miles north to Sawbridgeworth, and No 168 Squadron moved in on 30 November, remaining until 21 January 1944 with their cannon-armed Mk IAs and returning for a month's deployment on 3 March now flying Mk Is. Another Mustang squadron to utilise North Weald at this time was No 63, who stayed for ten days flying tactical reconnaissance sorties over enemy-held France and the Low Countries. Re-equipped with Super-marine Spitfire VBs, No 63 would return for a three-month stint the following year.

Following the departure of the two Norwegian squadrons in March 1944, North Weald was able, some five months later, to welcome airmen from another of the occupied European countries, Czechoslovakia, when Nos 310 and 312 Squadrons arrived from, respectively, Digby and Coltishall. No 234 Squadron RAF also touched down late that August. The units were tasked principally with fighter-reconnaissance missions, the Czech squadrons in their Spitfire IXs and No 234 initially with Spitfire VBs but straightaway beginning to convert to Mustangs.

No 310 Squadron's bomb-toting Spitfires were also involved in 'Ramrods'—short-range armed sorties to attack specific ground targets—and general support for USAAF bombers. Later the concentration turned to downing the V1 flying bombs ('doodlebugs') that were starting to appear with increasing regularity over the approaches to London. The Squadron completed its war by flying cover for the liberation of the Channel Isles in the summer of 1945. It was disbanded in Czechoslovakia in August the following year.

No 312 Squadron was based at North Weald for a mere five weeks, from August to October 1944. The Squadron flew sorties similar to those of its sister-unit, supporting USAAF bombers and RAF transports during the Arnhem campaign. The third Czech unit, No 313 Squadron, replaced

NORTH AMERICAN MUSTANG
Mks I and IA
Type: Fighter-reconnaissance aircraft
Engine: One 1,220hp Allison V-1710 inline
Length: 32ft 3in (9.83m)
Wing span: 37ft 0in (11.28m)
Weight: 8,800lb (3,990kg) loaded
Speed: 387mph (623kph) maximum
Range: 350 miles (565km)
Armament: Six 0.303in Browning machine guns or (Mk IA) four 20mm cannon
Crew: Pilot only

No 310 (Czechoslovak) Squadron

Motto
We Fight to Rebuild

Equipment
Supermarine Spitfire Mk IX (1944)

Below Artwork illustrating a Spitfire Mk IX of No 332 Squadron, 1944.

Left: A cannon-armed Mustang Mk IA in the colours of No 168 Squadron, which served at North Weald in late 1943 and again in February–March 1944.
Right: Spitfire Mk VB EP644 of No 313 Squadron is refuelled and rearmed at dispersal at North Weald in the second half of 1944.
Below: Spitfire VB 'AZ-W' of No 234 Squadron in the late summer of 1944, wearing black and white D-Day 'invasion stripes' on its undersurfaces.

No 312 (Czechoslovak) Squadron

Motto
Non Multi sed Multa
('Not Many Men but Many Deeds')

Equipment
Supermarine Spitfire Mk IX
(1944)

Below: A Spitfire H.F. Mk IX—notice the increased area of the rudder—flown from North Weald by Flight Lieutenant Otto Smik of No 312 Squadron in the autumn of 1944.

No 312 but was able to fly few sorties as the winter began to close in, and it departed in December.

No 234 Squadron arrived more or less concurrently with the Czech units but rapidly relinquished its Spitfire Mk Vs in favour of North American Mustang Mk IIIs—Merlin-engined and equivalent to the USAAF's P-51B—in October 1944, enabling much longer bomber escort missions to be flown.

In addition to these units, North Weald was host to a large number of other squadrons throughout 1944 and until the close of hostilities in Europe, all of them staying only briefly, some for a matter of days only. These many visitors are summarised in the table overleaf, their rôles during the final eighteen months of World War II—reconnaissance; short-range escort and ground attack; and then longer-range escort and ground-attack—reflecting the Allies' evolving requirements as the Germans were first evaluated, then attacked in occupied France and the Low Countries, and then increasingly pulverised as they were gradually driven back into their homeland.

The end of hostilities in 1945 and the repatriation of prisoners-of-war saw the return to North Weald of many faces well known in the Services. There can be few more recognisable than that of Group Captain Douglas Bader, whose prowess as a fighter leader, despite his disablities, is well known. Having been incarcerated as a POW in the notorious Colditz Castle for nearly four years, Bader returned to service as CO of the Fighter Command Sector headquarters at North Weald in July 1945. Allocated his 'personal' Spitfire IX, RK917 (coded 'D-B'), Bader was to lead the victory flypast over London on 15 September 1945, exactly five years after the recognised Battle of Britain Day, when, in 1940, the aerial confrontation

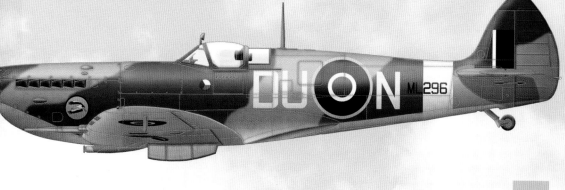

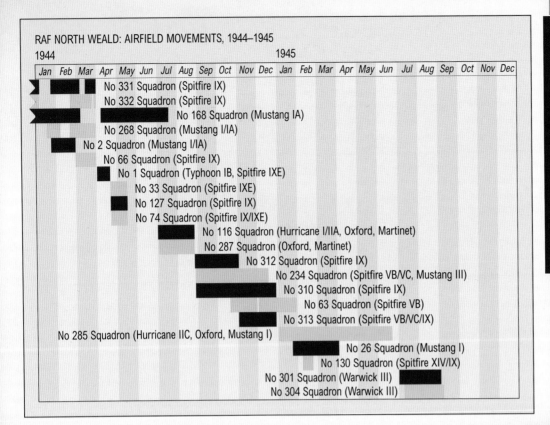

RAF NORTH WEALD: AIRFIELD MOVEMENTS, 1944–1945

1944												1945											
Jan	Feb	Mar	Apr	May	Jun	Jul	Aug	Sep	Oct	Nov	Dec	Jan	Feb	Mar	Apr	May	Jun	Jul	Aug	Sep	Oct	Nov	Dec

No 331 Squadron (Spitfire IX)
No 332 Squadron (Spitfire IX)
No 168 Squadron (Mustang IA)
No 268 Squadron (Mustang I/IA)
No 2 Squadron (Mustang I/IA)
No 66 Squadron (Spitfire IX)
No 1 Squadron (Typhoon IB, Spitfire IXE)
No 33 Squadron (Spitfire IXE)
No 127 Squadron (Spitfire IX)
No 74 Squadron (Spitfire IX/IXE)
No 116 Squadron (Hurricane I/IIA, Oxford, Martinet)
No 287 Squadron (Oxford, Martinet)
No 312 Squadron (Spitfire IX)
No 234 Squadron (Spitfire VB/VC, Mustang III)
No 310 Squadron (Spitfire IX)
No 63 Squadron (Spitfire VB)
No 313 Squadron (Spitfire VB/VC/IX)
No 285 Squadron (Hurricane IIC, Oxford, Mustang I)
No 26 Squadron (Mustang I)
No 130 Squadron (Spitfire XIV/IX)
No 301 Squadron (Warwick III)
No 304 Squadron (Warwick III)

AIRSPEED OXFORD Mk II
Type: Pilot and gunlaying trainer
Engine: Two 370hp Armstrong Siddeley Cheetah X radials
Length: 34ft 6in (10.52m)
Wing span: 53ft 4in (16.26m)
Weight: 7,600lb (3,450kg) loaded
Speed: 188mph (300kph) maximum
Service ceiling: 19,500ft (5,950m)
Armament: None
Crew: Three (pilot, instructor and wireless operator)

Below, left: Through 1944 and 1945, Spitfires and Mustangs were the most numerous aircraft types flying from North Weald. This is a Mustang Mk 1 of No 2 Squadron.

AD HOC COLLECTION

No 234 Squadron
Motto
Ognem Mortemque Despuimus
('We Spit Fire and Death')
Equipment
Supermarine Spitfire Mk VC (1944), North American Mustang Mk III (1944)

was said to have reached its height. Taking off from North Weald, Bader led a formation of eleven pilots who had fought in that battle—a formation which in turn made up the vanguard for more than 300 warplanes flying over the bomb-ravaged city of London in salute.

The date 15 September was to be celebrated for many years after the war by means of RAF Battle of Britain air shows, initially at almost every active service airfield: Suffolk alone, for example, had Open Days at Wattisham, Felixstowe and Honington on the same day in 1954. Repeated over many succeeding years, the commemoration eventually succumbed to a lack of enthusiasm and funding from the authorities at the Ministry, and the date is today celebrated in this fashion only at RAF Leuchars in Fife, where, with due reverence, those who gave their lives during the

Below: A Mustang Mk III of No 234 Squadron, with the revised 'Malcolm hood' cockpit canopy.

Right: Profile of a Mustang Mk 1 of No 26 Squadron, which was stationed at North Weald as the war in Europe drew to a close.

battle are always remembered by an air show on the Saturday nearest 15 September.

For many of the aircrew, groundcrew and other RAF personnel who participated in the 1939–45 conflict, North Weald proved to be their last home. The service that they gave, and the sacrifice that they made, must never be forgotten.

Right: Group Captain Douglas Bader, the famous 'legless pilot', with RAF personnel at North Weald in September 1945.

No 285 Squadron

Motto
Respice Finem
('Consider the End')

Equipment
Airspeed Oxford Mk II (1945), Hawker Hurricane Mk IIC (1945), North American Mustang Mk I (1945)

Right: RAF North Weald, showing the general layout at the close of hostilities. The runways and peritrack have been extended, and there are much improved facilties for dispersal. thanks largely to further extensions of the site to the north and west

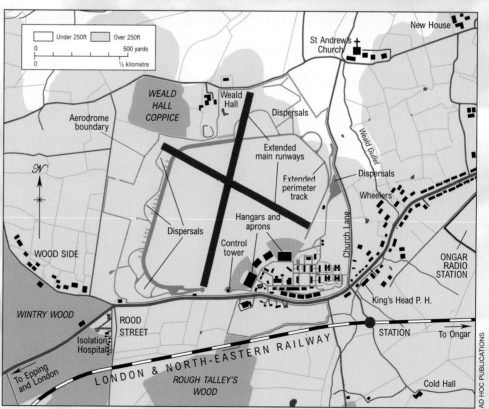

COLD WAR JETS

WITH the defeat of Nazi Germany in May 1945 came radical changes in the structure of the RAF and, as a result, of North Weald aerodrome. The Norwegians had gone, and many RAF fighter squadrons had either found a new home or faced disbandment. In an extreme change, North Weald ceased being a Fighter Command station and instead came under the ægis of RAF Transport Command with the arrival of two squadrons of Vickers Warwicks, Nos 301 and 304, both crewed by Poles who had escaped from their home country on occupation and found their way to Britain to fly in the RAF. Initially bomber squadrons operating Handley Page Halifaxes (No 301) and Vickers Wellingtons (No 304), the two units now undertook regular communication flights to and from Italy and other liberated European countries, although later their operations were restricted to the United Kingdom. Both squadrons ultimately converted to Halifax C.VIII transports before ceasing operations in December 1946. Neither unit was allocated an official RAF crest, although the aircraft bore Polish insignia, comprising the coat of arms of Pomerania (No 301 Squadron) and a stylised flying bomb (No 304).

On 1 November 1946 No 695 Squadron arrived at North Weald for a detachment lasting until April 1947. Equipped with Spitfire XVI, Vultee Vengeance and Airspeed Oxford aircraft, the Squadron was tasked with providing targets and supporting anti-aircraft co-operation. One of 695's claims to fame was that it was the highest-numbered unit ever to have served in the RAF.

Flying came to a halt at North Weald in April 1947 but the Station was for a period home to the Aircrew Selection Centre. The airfield was very busy again in June 1948, however, as a result of a national dock strike. Many thousands of troops, with motor vehicles, were billeted at the site while they carried out the essential loading and off-loading at London Docks. The exercise had to be repeated a year later when a further dispute erupted.

The year 1949 saw the airfield reactivated as a flying station under the authority of RAF Fighter Command and

No 695 Squadron

Motto
We Exercise Their Arms

Equipment
Supermarine Spitfire Mk XVIE (1946–1947), Vultee Vengeance Mk IV (1946–1947), Airspeed Oxford Mks I and II (1946–1947), North American Harvard T. Mk IIB (1946–1947), Miles Martinet Mk I (1946–1947)

Below: A Warwick C.III. Aircraft of this type served at North Weald briefly in summer 1945.

Right: A Supermarine Spitfire L. F. Mk XVIE in the markings of No 695 Squadron while resident at North Weald.

Below, right: An aerial photograph of North Weald aerodrome taken in 1947, its layout a far cry from that familiar to the personnel of No 39 Squadron thirty years earlier. Further extensions to the main runways involved, as can clearly be seen, the breaching of Weald Hall Lane, which as a result was split into two no-through roads. Yet more upgrading was to follow.

VICKERS WARWICK C. Mk III
Type: Long-range transport
Engines: Two 1,850hp Pratt & Whitney Double Wasp R-2800 radials
Length: 70ft 6in (21.49m)
Wing span: 96ft 8½in (29.48m)
Weight: 46,000lb (20,860kg) loaded
Speed: 260mph (420kph) max.
Range: 2,150 miles (3,460km)
Service ceiling: 15,000ft (4,920m)
Payload: 6,700lb (3,040kg)
Crew: Four

SUPERMARINE SPITFIRE L.F. Mk XVI
Type: Fighter/fighter-bomber
Engine: One 1,720hp Packard Merlin inline
Length: 31ft 4in (9.55m)
Wing span: 32ft 8in (9.96m)
Speed: 405mph (652kph) max.
Range: 980 miles (1,580km) max.
Armament: Two 20mm cannon plus two 0.50cal machine guns, plus up to 1,000lb (454kg) bombs or rockets.
Crew: Pilot only

thus commenced another important era in North Weald's history. Re-forming after the war as Auxiliary Air Force squadrons at RAF Hendon in 1946 and flying Spitfire L. F. Mk XVIEs, Nos 601 and 604 Squadrons quite quickly found themselves crowded out from north London and were detailed to take up new lodgings at North Weald. No 601 arrived on 27 March 1949 and No 604 the following day. For both it was a return to old haunts, No 604 having served at the Essex station for a few days in 1939 and a few months after the outbreak of war, and 601 having made for a brief stopover back in 1925. Both units were immediately marked down to receive the new Vampire jet fighter as part of the North Weald Wing.

The De Havilland Vampire arrived in service at North Weald amid much enthusiasm, firstly equipping Nos 601 and 604 Squadrons with the

COURTESY NWAM

67

COURTESY PHILIP JARRETT

Left: Preparing to start the Merlin engine of a No 604 Squadron Spitfire Mk 16e. The years 1948–49 saw a number of 'cosmetic' changes to the RAF inventory: arabic designations supplanted roman; camouflage was discarded in favour of silver finishes for fighter aircraft; and national markings were redesigned. Below: Profiles depicting a Spitfire L.F.16e of No 604 Squadron in camouflage paint and a 601 Squadron Spitfire L.F.16e in silver overall.

F.3 version from November 1949. The North Weald Wing was brought to full strength in March the following year with the arrival of No 72 Squadron, its sole full-time component. No 72 was initially flying the F.3 also, but quickly passed some of its aircraft on to the two Auxiliary units as it was in the process of re-equipping with the F.B.5 fighter/ground-attack version of the jet.

Always a very popular aircraft with its aircrew, the twin-boomed Vampire was, at this stage in its career, the most successful British aircraft design from the point of view of overseas sales. It was likened in many ways to the Spitfire in its handling—an accolade indeed when one realises that the squadrons of the early 1950s were often led and manned by pilots who had flown Spitfires during the war and that they, better than anyone, could make the comparison. However, in order to highlight a fault afflicting the first-generation Vampires—and a fault that was characteristic of so many of the early British jet aircraft—one had only to consider their endurance. The problem was remedied in later marks of the aircraft with the addition of wing-mounted fuel tanks, which were able to extend its range to some 1,150 miles.

No 601 (County of London) Squadron

Motto
None authorised

Equipment
Supermarine Spitfire L. F. Mk 16e (1949). De Havilland Vampire F. Mk 3 (1949–1952), Gloster Meteor F. Mk 8 (1952–1957)

Right: The personnel of No 601 Squadron outside one of the main hangars at North Weald, circa 1952.

Below: North Weald 'At Home' brochure, 17 September 1949 —with the Spitfire still, seemingly, the aircraft of importance.

Below, right: General support duties at RAF Stations were carried out by the Station Flight, which comprised a small group of miscellaneous aircraft. Amongst those at North Weald was this Airspeed Oxford Mk 2, seen here passing the old control tower in 1952.

COURTESY JAMES IVERS/601 SQUADRON ASSN

OFFICIAL PROGRAMME
BY PERMISSION OF THE AIR COUNCIL

ROYAL AIR FORCE STATION, NORTH WEALD
"AT HOME"
SATURDAY, 17th SEPTEMBER, 1949

Below: The transition from propellers to jets: arrival day for the first of No 601's Vampires —VT864 is nearest—with a Spitfire Mk 16 framing the photograph at left. The tall building behind and between the two main hangars is the water tower.

Always in competition with the contemporary Gloster Meteor, which was soon to re-equip the North Weald Wing, the Vampire quickly came to be thought of as a ground-attack aircraft rather than an air-defence interceptor; indeed, with the arrival on the scene of the F.B.5, powered by a much improved Goblin III (D. Gn 3) engine, it was viewed exclusively in this light. The aircraft, in two-seat configuration, was also for many years the mainstay of the RAF's training programme, converting pilots who had been awarded their 'Wings' on Harvards to the more demanding tasks involved in flying jet fighters.

COURTESY NWAM

COURTESY JAMES IVERS/601 SQUADRON ASSN

In the early 1950s the military mind remembered recent times of war; additional anxieties were the far-off conflict in Korea, and at the forefront was the speedy rise of the Soviet Union as a military superpower. Because of these influences, Britain continually trained for war. Military exercises were very frequent, involving not only Regular serving personnel but also the auxiliary flying units and part-time troops. The United Kingdom was full of airfields and aircraft at the time, and North Weald was a vital component in the Defence of the Realm. Weekend battle-exercises against European and US forces, for example, were commonplace, and during the practice interceptions mounted by Fighter Command the skies of East Anglia thundered to the sound of hundreds of jet engines. The life of a fighter pilot was a busy one, as was that of each of his groundcrew.

The Auxiliary squadrons, manned as they were by part-time volunteers, could not receive the intensive training enjoyed by their full-time

Above: Vampire Mk 3s of No 601 Squadron are put through their paces.

Below, left: Originally housed in the main hangars at North Weald, the Auxiliaries were later moved to separate accommodation on the western side of the airfield, using hangars formerly sited at nearby Matching Green (a wartime USAAF base). Here members of No 601 are in conversation; Station CO Wing Commander Al Deere OBE DSO DFC, the distinguished wartime pilot, is on the right, facing right, hands in pockets. The building shown survives today.

Above: A close view of one of No 601's Vampires, showing the squadron emblem and aircraft code letter on the nose.

COURTESY JAMES IVERS/601 SQUADRON ASSOCIATION

No 604 (County of London) Squadron

Motto
Sic Vis Pacem Para Bellum
('If One Wants Peace, Prepare for War')

Equipment
Bristol Blenheim Mk IF (1939–1940), Supermarine Spitfire L. F. Mk 16e (1949), De Havilland Vampire F. Mk 3 (1949–1952), Gloster Meteor F. Mk 8 (1952–1957)

Right, top: New for old: three of No 604 Squadron's Vampires, as yet unadorned with unit markings, await their pilots along the eastern perimeter track following their delivery to North Weald in late 1949. Some of the Squadron's camouflaged Spitfire 16s are seen in the background.

Right, above: Profiles depicting Vampire 3s of No 601 (upper) and 604 (lower) Squadrons, showing the striking *décor* adopted later in the units' time on type.

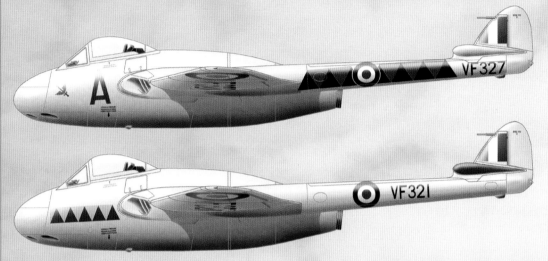

counterparts in the RAF, but the annual Summer Camps offered them opportunities of working with other units, conducting live firing exercises and generally honing their skills. They were much looked forward to, not least because they often took place in exotic climes. No 601 found themselves at Sylt, an island off Germany, and Ta Kali in Malta during their period at North Weald, while 604 were sent to Ta Kali and to Thorney Island near Portsmouth (proving that you cannot win them all!).

Right: A pair of No 601 Squadron's Vampires gets airborne during Summer Camp exercises in Malta.

COURTESY TOM DOCHERTY/No 72 SQUADRON ASSN

Left: The arrival from Odiham of No 72 Squadron on 22 March 1950 marked the stationing at North Weald of a full-time Fighter Command squadron for the first time since the war. Their Vampire 3s carried their wartime-type, three-letter recognition codes clustered together on the nose.

COURTESY TOM DOCHERTY/No 72 SQUADRON ASSN

Left: 'Scrambles' were still very much on the agenda in 1950, as demonstrated here by pilots of No 72 Squadron during Exercise 'Emperor' in October 1950. The aircraft are now Vampire Mk 5s, and a redesign of the *décor* is evident, with the unit crest, flanked by red-outlined blue bars, borne in miniature on the nose and the individual aircraft identity letter worn on the nosewheel door and—though not visibly here—on the tail boom.

COURTESY TOM DOCHERTY/No 72 SQUADRON ASSN

DE HAVILLAND VAMPIRE F. Mk 3

Type: Interceptor fighter
Engine: One 3,100lb thrust De Havilland Goblin 2 turbojet
Length: 30ft 9in (9.37m)
Wing span: 40ft 0in (12.19m)
Speed: 530mph (850kph) max.
Range: 1,145 miles (1,840km) max.
Armament: Four 20mm Hispano cannon.
Crew: Pilot only

Left: The markings described above were short-lived, and code letters were soon appearing large on the nose, with the Squadron crest moved to the forward nosewheel door. The overall finish of the airframe was High Speed Silver.

Right: Pre-flight maintenance in the field at North Weald for No 72 Squadron's Vampire F.B.5 VZ260/'Z'. Drop tanks were available to these aircraft, significantly increasing range and particularly useful for long-distance ferry flights.

COURTESY TOM DOCHERTY/No 72 SQUADRON ASSN

Below, right: A profile of a No 72 Squadron Vampire F. B. Mk 5 based at North Weald in late 1950.

No 72 Squadron

Motto
Swift

Equipment
De Havilland Vampire F. Mk 3 (1950), De Havilland Vampire F. B. Mk 5 (1950–1952), Gloster Meteor F. Mk 8 (1952–1953)

The overriding threat of a nuclear attack brought changes to the infrastructure of command and control in the region, too. The Control Room at Blake Hall became redundant, left behind by the requirements of more modern technology. A new nuclear attack-proof underground bunker, disguised as a bungalow, was built at Kelvedon Hatch some ten miles to the south-east of the airfield and furnished to act as the Central Control Unit for the Metropolitan area. From here, intrusions by the Soviet Union were monitored, fighters scrambled and interceptions controlled. Should the 'Cold War', as Churchill described it, ever have become 'hot', the nuclear defence of the city and suburbs would also have been overseen from here.

'I'm Going for a Coffee'

Leading Aircraftman John Meddows, No 72 Squadron

It was 30 June 1952, although the precise time in the morning escapes me, but four Vampires were taxying down to the northern end of the runway in preparation for take-off, and, having always been fascinated by the sight and sound of multiple departures, I paused for a few minutes to see them away. They turned, and everything appeared to be normal as they gathered speed, but then one of the two leading aircraft failed to rise and ploughed through the boundary hedge bordering the airfield, crossed the Epping–Ongar road and finished up in the field just yards from the old Kia-Ora Café.

It was at this point that I was joined by Flight Sergeant Todd, who suggested that I had better get up there. Fortunately, the engine of my motorcycle was still warm, and I was on the scene in just a few minutes, where I found Flight Lieutenant Clayton endeavouring to slide the canopy back and unstrap himself. This was achieved with a little help from me, and he climbed out of the cockpit amid the kerosene vapour starting to pour from the engine. I do not ever remember having met such a cool character, who then handed his helmet and mask to me and said, 'Tell the CO I'm going

for a coffee in the Mess,' and just walked off as if his experience had been something that happened every day.

An investigation of the aircraft found that the accident could be ascribed to a fundamental error: one of the intake blanks had not been removed!

JIM DOLDER, COURTESY JOHN MEDDOWS

Right: The remains of No 72 Squadron's Vampire 'F', which failed to get airborne from North Weald on 30 June 1952. Luckily, the pilot was able to walk away.

Prangs and Bangs

Senior Aircraftman Geoff Monahan, No 72 Squadron

The Royal Air Force of the early 1950s consisted, in part, of a large number of National Servicemen. On call-up I arrived at Innsworth in Gloucestershire for eight weeks of drill (or 'square-bashing', as it was known). As the time drew to a close, it was suggested that I become a typist, with the bribe that I would become a Leading Aircraftsman in six months. The appeal of this 'trade' was somewhat limited to my mind, and so instead I applied to become an armourer. My request fell on deaf ears, the reason being, I was informed, that I wore glasses. I explained that I wanted to work on the guns not fire them, and the production of a First Class certificate gained in the ATC (which entitled me to choose my trade) saw me off to Kirkham in Lancashire for three months' training. So it was that, in early April 1952, I arrived at North Weald.

Above: Gloster Meteor Mk 8 WK749 of No 72 Squadron, probably at North Weald. This is one of the aircraft involved in the fatal accident over Great Totham, near Chelmsford, on 17 October 1952. The name of the pilot depicted is not known.

I was under the impression that my two fellow-travellers and I would be posted to No 601 Squadron, so we reported to Flight Lieutenant Mason, who was later to command No 72 Squadron. He somewhat grudgingly allocated us quarters in No 601 Squadron's billets and we settled for the night. It was with some surprise that, the very next day, I was allocated to No 72 Squadron, so my first posting to No 601 was short. Perhaps they heard us coming.

No 72 Squadron were dispersed near the church on the north-eastern side of the airfield and our first walk to the Squadron was interrupted that day by the arrival on the cross runway of a No 601 Squadron Vampire, the port undercarriage leg of which promptly collapsed on landing, although no injury ensued. (It is noteworthy that this Vampire, VT812, lives on in the colours of No 601 Squadron at the RAF Museum, Hendon.) In another incident later during my time at North Weald, Station Commander Wing Commander Al Deere borrowed a No 72 Squadron Vampire on an air firing exercise. Unfortunately he skidded off the runway on take off and ended up in a ditch. A colleague and I had the job of disarming it—not an easy task given the aircraft's position.

The North Weald armourers were headed by a firm-but-fair Warrant Officer named Churchill. If anyone had a gripe against an armourer, they had to deal with W/O Churchill first. The fair side of him was seen in the way that, if work allowed, we could go off early: we could pick up our passes at the guard house and were free until the next work-day. On one occasion I remember that, on being asked for our pass-outs, we were told that we could not leave as it was not yet 4 p.m. On being challenged with 'You had better speak to Warrant Officer Churchill', our passes were handed out immediately.

In a tragic incident in July 1952, the CO of No 72 Squadron, Squadron Leader C. L. C. Mason, was working up an aerobatic team of four Vampires. Returning from practice one lunchtime, the pilots attempted a formation roll over the airfield—but too low, too slow! Two aircraft crashed on the airfield and their occupants, Flight Lieutenant Wyborn and Sergeant Randall, were killed; both are interred in the churchyard at St Andrew's. Later in my time with No 72 Squadron, W/O Churchill was to lead me and a group of other volunteers in the gruesome task of guarding the crash-site of two Meteors, WK690 and WK749, that had collided over Great Totham in Essex. One ejection seat, complete with the unfortunate pilot, had landed outside the back

door of a house owned by a lady whilst another large piece of wreckage was to be found in a garden where the owner was very unhappy at our intention of removing it: he had already called the Press, who were on their way to photograph him with it. We still removed it! Flying Officer Charles Muldownie and Pilot Officer Ian Carmichael were the pilots who lost their lives on that occasion. Muldownie was an experienced pilot, a Squadron Leader during the wartime years, with over 2,500 hours in his logbook.

With the transfer of No 72 Squadron to Church Fenton in May 1953 came both promotion and a move for me—albeit only across the airfield to the Station Armoury, where, with a change of RAF procedure, all North Weald armoury maintenance was to be carried out. Ammunition would be delivered in steel boxes by rail into a siding at North Weald station, from where we would collect it and take it to the bomb dump. We would draw our needs from there, as and when required. The promotion meant that my weekly pay-packet was now a healthy thirteen shillings a day, which, with board, food, uniform and travel warrants all found, was not as bad as it sounds.

Below: The wreckage of Meteor WK690 under guard. The early days of Meteor flying saw huge numbers of accidents, a large percentage of them, sadly, fatal.

Right: A brand new Meteor 8 for No 601 Squadron; notice the Squadron emblem, in red, on the engine nacelle. The aircraft is fitted with the standard underbelly conformal fuel tank, for extra range.

Below: A Meteor F. Mk 8 on the strength of No 72 Squadron, in 1952, This aircraft was that usually flown by the CO, Squadron Leader C. L. C. Mason, specially marked with a blue fin and an appropriate code letter. Bottom: No 72 Squadron's Meteors on the line at North Weald. The famous radio masts are clear to see. Situated only a mile or so to the east of the airfield, they were viewed with mixed feelings: while they were useful landmarks for arriving pilots, they on the other hand presented something of a low-flying hazard, particularly in inclement weather.

The year 1952 was a significant one as it marked the arrival at North Weald of a different type of aircraft. The Wing converted to the Gloster Meteor F.8, a much bulkier beast than the Vampire with which it had fulfilled its task for the past three or four years. Conversion was helped by the fact that, during the Vampire years, there being no two-seat trainer at this time, each squadron had two of its own Meteor T.7 trainers to enable dual checks to be carried out. This meant that many if not all of the Vampire pilots had had Meteor experience before the new single-seaters arrived.

July 23 saw the arrival of the first three jets for No 72 Squadron, and the full allocation was on strength by the end of August. The two Auxiliary squadrons were also re-equipped with the aircraft, No 601 Squadron taking delivery of their first three on 11 August and being completely re-equipped by the 18th, and No 604 receiving their first Meteor on 25 August and having a full complement by 15 September.

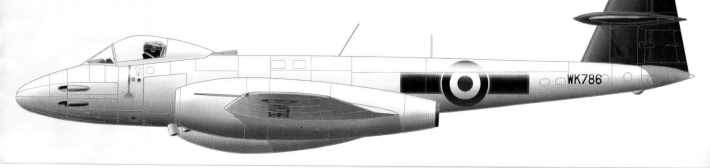

WK786

TOM MOULSON, COURTESY JAMES IVER/601 SQUADRON ASSN

COURTESY JAMES IVER/601 SQUADRON ASSN

Left, upper: Two aircrewmen prepare for a flight in a Meteor T.7 at North Weald. Notice the World War II-style headgear: 'bone domes' were not yet part of the flying kit in the early 1950s.

Left, lower: Members of No 601 Squadron inspect a flag target after firing practice during Summer Camp on Malta. Each participating pilot would fire rounds tipped in different-coloured paint, enabling scores to be assessed. Some of the Squadron's Meteor 8s are in the background.

Below: The cockpit of a Meteor Mk 8.

From the pilots' point of view, the Meteor F.8 should have been a much safer aircraft than earlier marks of the *genre* with the fitting of a Martin-Baker ejection seat in this version, but the 'good to fly—easy to die' reputation of the Meteor lived on, and crashes involving the aircraft continued to plague the RAF. The North Weald Wing did not escape the carnage. The aircraft had an abysmal single-engine performance, and far too many single-engine approaches ended in tragedy.

Below: As in No 72 Squadron, No 601's CO flew a distinctive Meteor, in this instance one with its tailfin adorned in black and red stripes. Uniquely at North Weald, No 601 painted the cannon fairings of their Meteors red for a period.

Right: A No 601 Squadron Meteor is refuelled and re-armed during Summer Camp. Notice the smudging caused by blast gases around the muzzle trough of the port lower cannon. Below: Season's greetings from the County of Middlesex Squadron.

COURTESY NWAM

COURTESY NWAM

GLOSTER METEOR F. Mk 8
Type: Interceptor fighter
Engine: Two 3,600lb thrust Rolls-Royce Derwent 8 turbo-jets
Length: 44ft 7in (13.59m)
Wing span: 37ft 2in (11.33m)
Speed: 600mph (966kph) max.
Range: 980 miles (1,580km) max.
Armament: Four 20mm Hispano cannon.
Crew: Pilot only

July 1953 saw No 72 Squadron depart from North Weald for the final time, having been posted to Church Fenton for a few months before moving to Leconfield in Yorkshire. This move proved to be the prelude to the final, great chapter in Royal Air Force history at North Weald.

On 2 December 1953 No 111 Squadron—'Treble One'—once again took up residence at North Weald, re-forming as a unit having been disbanded some six and a half years previously. Flying the Meteor F.8, the Squadron was led at the time by Squadron Leader Harry Pears DFC, who by coincidence had test-flown and accepted the very first Meteor F.8 to join the Service. Under Pears the unit maintained the heavy workload left by No 72 Squadron, co-operating fully with their colleagues in the two Royal Auxiliary Air Force squadrons, including the armed practice camps when pilots got the chance to use their ammunition against towed flag targets. In 1954 this camp took place at Acklington in Northumberland and, while in progress, witnessed the arrival on No 111 of Squadron

Below: A Meteor 8 in the colours of No 604 Squadron flying from North Weald.

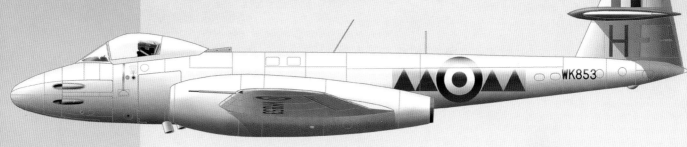

Right: A view of Meteor 8 WK744/'G' of No 601 Squadron, its code letter presented in black with a silver outline on the red nosewheel door. By early 1954 silver-finished Fighter Command aircraft were becoming a thing of the past once more, as camouflage paintwork began to be re-introduced. Here underwing drop tanks supplement the external belly tank to permit maximum range.

COURTESY NWAM

Leader Roger Topp AFC. With Pears moving on, the Squadron returned to North Weald in February 1954 with Topp at the helm.

'Treble One' was one of the last squadrons in RAF Fighter Command to be equipped with the Meteor as a front-line day fighter; such was the measure of the perceived threat from the Soviet Bloc that by this time the Command had under its authority some thirty squadrons flying the type. One significant upgrade had been introduced—the replacement of the original metal hood with a clear-view canopy, affording pilots a much improved rearward view from the cockpit. The aircraft, however, had one particular, and insoluble, problem in its rôle as an interceptor: its quarry the bomber aircraft, as indeed clearly demonstrated by the RAF's own Canberra force let alone the enemy's, was operating at higher and higher altitudes and the Meteor simply did not have the performance to match. Its climb rate was insufficient and its manœuvrability at height sorely lacking. These shortcomings provided the impetus for the urgent replacement programme that was in full swing at the time, which brought into service both the disappointing Supermarine Swift and the superlative

Above: Gloster Meteor Mk 8s of No 604 Squadron on the flight line at North Weald, with the nearby radio masts again in evidence in the background. Unlike sister-squadron No 601, No 604 did not display their unit crest on the engine nacelles of their aircraft.

Above: No 111 Squadron's Meteors arrived at North Weald already wearing their camouflage paintwork. The scheme was standard throughout the Command, although there were variations in the pattern. The undersurfaces remained silver. Left: One of No 111's Meteors is refuelled from a bowser, both the fuselage tanks and the ventral tank receiving replenishment. The Squadron had 22 Meteor F.8s on strength and one two-seat Meteor T.7—and no fewer than 37 pilots!

JOHN BEAUMONT, COURTESY ARTHUR MORETON

Above: No more silver: a close-up of a 604 Squadron Meteor in the new camouflaged finish. Notice the red triangle warning of the presence of an ejection seat,
Right: No 111 Squadron Meteor pilots pose for a photograph outside their hangar at North Weald.

COURTESY NWAM

Above: The North Weald Tiger Moth—'of uncertain ownership'—looking very sprightly with its red and white chequers.

Hawker Hunter. For the moment, however, No 111 Squadron worked up with its Meteors, and was declared fully operational on 7 March 1954. A year and more of intensive 1950s-style fighter training followed, until in June 1955 the Squadron began to take delivery of the aircraft with which it will for ever be associated.

The introduction of the Hawker Hunter represented a very significant milestone in the evolution of RAF Fighter Command: the aircraft was the first wholly successful indigenous swept-wing fighter, the first British-built RAF fighter capable of exceeding the speed of sound (albeit in a dive) and, for a period, the World Speed Record holder. It was not without its teething troubles when first introduced into service, but by the time No 111 Squadron received their sixteen Hunters the design's foibles had been successfully addressed and the Mk 4 was the

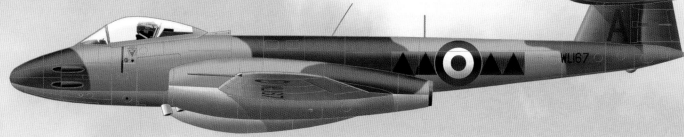

Above: The Auxiliary squadrons' Meteors also began to appear in drab camouflage, as depicted here covering one of No 601's Meteors. The bright unit markings were, however, retained: *espirit de corps* was of immense importance in the RAF.
Right: Royal Auxiliary Air Force Meteors lined up for inspection at North Weald in 1954 by Air Vice-Marshal The Earl of Bandon GBE CB DSO AFC, accompanied by Station CO Group Captain G. C. Eversleigh OBE AFC.

COURTESY NWAM

JOHN BEAUMONT, COURTESY ARTHUR MORETON

standard version. Equipped with a quartet of 30mm Aden cannon and capable of flying at altitudes around 50,000 feet, it could hold its own with the very best in the world.

Some years previously in No 111 Squadron, the then CO, Squadron Leader John Gillan, had set a speed record in his Hurricane, flying from Edinburgh to London in 48 minutes on 10 February 1938 at an average 408mph (aided by a following wind). The arrival of the Hunter suggested that a similar demonstration might be achieved, and so to illustrate the prowess of the current squadron Roger Topp flew WT739 from London to Edinburgh in 27 minutes 52.8 seconds, at an average speed of 717.5mph, thereby ensuring that this particular record continued to feature in the No 111 Squadron annals. It was eventually broken, some thirty years later, by a supersonic Phantom.

Left, upper: No 111 Squadron Meteor groundcrewmen in relaxed mood.
Above: Oxygen replenishment for one of No 111 Squadron's Meteors.

Below: The arrival of the Hunter did not see the complete disappearance of the Meteor from the No 111 Squadron inventory: a two-seat T.7 trainer was retained for general duties.

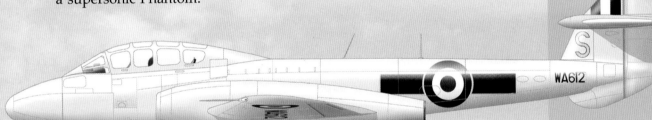

Below: Four Hunter Mk 4s of No 111 Squadron head earthwards.

No 111 (F) Squadron

Motto
Adstantes ('Standing By')

Equipment
Hawker Hurricane Mk I (1940),
Supermarine Spitfire Mk VB
(1941), Gloster Meteor F. Mk 8
(1953–1955), Hawker Hunter
F. Mk 4/Mk 6 (1955–1958)

EJECTION
SEAT

COURTESY NWAM

Before long, and not for the first (or indeed last) time, the influence of the late Sir Thomas Pike could be felt in North Weald's history. He had commanded No 219 Squadron (Blenheims and Beaufighters) at RAF Tangmere for six months in 1941 but the following year took over as the

Right, top: Flying Officer David Goodwin, a 'Treble-One' Hunter pilot, in his cockpit.
Above: A profile showing a Hunter 4 of No 111 Squadron. Coloured wing tips identified the various Flights within the Squadron.

Right: The layout of the aerodrome in the mid-1950s, showing the locations of the squadrons. The Aircraft Servicing Flight (ASF) was a vital part of the establishment, responsible for Major and Interim Inspections, repairs and modifications concerning the aircraft of all the squadrons—it was here that the main technical knowledge and skill resided. Notice the significant upgrading of main runways, peritracks and hardstandings required for the reception of the Hunter; in the far north, this involved the rerouting of Canes Lane. The plan is little changed today, except for the significant addition of the M11 motorway, which cuts through the western fringe.

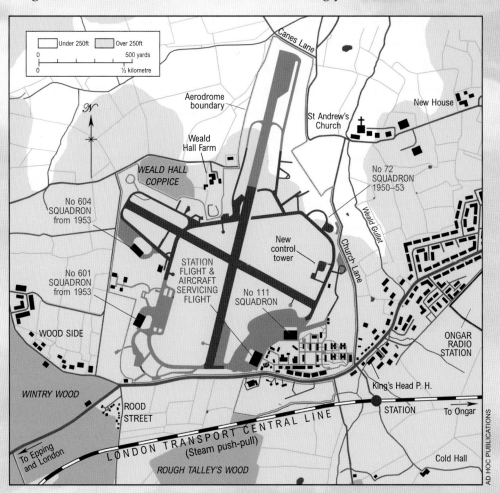

It's All Changed

Air Commodore Roger Topp AFC**

I was sitting in my office within the Squadron hangar at North Weald, gazing dreamily out of the window. On the airfield along the line of our parked Hunters the usual activities of ground crew and pilots were in full swing. It was a perfect September afternoon in 1956 and things were, I thought, going along very nicely.

About three weeks earlier I had returned from a trip to Canada and the US in a Hastings transport aircraft, and in a few days' time I would be repeating the journey—but this time I would be in my Hunter and leading six others. The RAF had been invited by the Royal Canadian Air Force to participate in the Toronto Air Show, a major international event. The Chief of Air Staff had accepted the invitation and, not surprisingly, had chosen to send the Hunter, the RAF's latest fighter aircraft; in turn, the C-in-C Fighter Command had decided that 'Treble One' should go. At that time, in 1956, we, together with No 43 Squadron at Leuchars, shared the RAF's formation aerobatic commitments and No 43 drew the short straw, so we joyfully planned to take our team of five aircraft and two spares across the Atlantic. Our aircraft were still resplendent in their camouflage and unique squadron markings; the 'Black Arrows' were yet to be so nominated.

The Hastings trip had had two objectives: first, to recce the route we would be using and meet all those who would be involved in helping us make the exercise a success; and secondly, to position spares at strategic airfields along the route. The Hastings would accompany the Hunters and be able to carry some further light spares. Its main payload then would be to carry our ground crew and their toolkits.

On the recce mission there were three passengers—the Station Commander, Group Captain Jamie Rankin, a Battle of Britain pilot, one-time scratch golfer and all-round good egg; Flight Lieutenant 'Chalky' White, a stalwart engineer; and myself. Our route was North Weald to Keflavik in Iceland, Bluie West One in Greenland, Goose Bay in Nova Scotia, Ottawa, Toronto, and—because the US had by now got into the act—via several US Air Force air bases and on to Washington, thence to Goose Bay and so back along the outward route to the United Kingdom. As well as at Toronto and Washington, we were to give displays at several other Canadian and US locations.

Jamie Rankin dealt with all the diplomatic protocol, 'Chalky' busied himself with matters of AVTAG and oxygen and the dropping-off of selected spares, while I spent most of my time in the Met offices and the ATCs. At every stop our hosts, the USAF, seemed fanatically determined to treat us to the best party we would ever be likely encounter: as we progressed along the route I began to doubt that even my party-hardened pilots would be able to survive this kind of hospitality.

Depositing our few spares in unlikely and remote spots was a sensitive issue. We would have been happier to have had them all with us on the Hastings, but the payload limits did not permit this. Neither was I happy about the shortage of spares. At the time the Hunter was still only recently in service and all squadrons suffered from shortages of spares, particularly of tyres and brake pads. The Dunlop 'Maxaret' braking system needed to be operated sensitively, particularly on wet/dry runways such as when puddles were interspersed with dry patches. It was relatively easy to lock the brakes momentarily, which would often be followed by the popping sound of the tyres bursting; and if one were the guilty party one had an uncomfortable awareness that derisory cheers would be emanating from the crew room. Fast landings on short runways also resulted in rapid brake-pad wear and Dunlop could not keep up with the demands for tyres and pads. Hard to come by, too, were spare Rolls-Royce Avon engines. We were allocated only one engine, and on that September afternoon it was somewhere in mid-Atlantic heading west on board a tramp freighter. A further concern was the VHF radio. At the time it was highly unreliable, and Forms 700 were littered with 'VHF u/s' comments; its range was also very limited. With our navigation aids consisting only of the P4 compass and a dodgy short-range VHF, facing long-stage legs mostly over the sea, often out of contact either with the destination or departure airfields (or, for that matter, with anyone else), we were likely to encounter some nail-biting experiences.

Above: The first team of 'aerobats': (left to right) Flying Officers Garret and Goodwin, Squadron Leader Topp (CO), Flight Lieutenant Aird and Flight Sergeant Beck, with a Hunter 4 as the backdrop.

During the recce we found that our USAF hosts along the route were amazed and non-comprehending that we did not have a 'Bird Dog' radio compass in the Hunter. It was standard equipment for all US aircraft and beacons were in plentiful supply wherever they were likely to operate. For some reason the RAF decided that their pilots did not need this valuable aid; after all, the Battle of Britain had been won without it, and therefore we, too, could continue to navigate by keeping a mental plot going throughout the sortie—feasible, perhaps, for the slower, piston-engine fighters but not practicable for fast, single-crew, single-engine, high-flying, limited-endurance jets flying long distances, often in or above complete cloud cover from take-off to landing.

On 'Treble One' we had already experienced frustratingly long periods of R/T silence and hence no nav aid during long transit flights over continental Europe, particularly whenever over flying France. We were supposed to make our way via the French ATC system by calling them on the VHF emergency frequency, 121.5Mc/s. Even if the ground operators heard our short-range bleats, they often did not reply, perhaps because we were using the English language but more likely because, while we might have sounded stressed, we were not (they probably thought) *in* distress because we were not calling 'Mayday'. Once we flew Tangmere–Bordeaux above complete cloud cover without a squeak from the ATC and finally let down on Flight Plan, not a million miles from the towering Pyrenees, but fortunately broke through cloud at about 15,000 feet. Similar experiences occurred en route to Milan and to Zürich.

Even at home it only had to be seriously 'claggy' throughout the country to hear numerous plaintive calls from Hunter pilots across the skies attempting to sound unstressed as they pleaded for 'check steers' and QGH descents. To us it seemed that the powers above were determined to make matters difficult for us rather than easy. How the babble would have been quelled if we had all had a 'Bird Dog'! It was a long time before DME arrived, in the Lightning.

My mind turned back to our Atlantic trip. The Met offices at the three staging bases we would be calling at all emphasised that, as we would be going through in September/October, they would be liable to rapid changes from fine weather to dense fog; it only required a degree or two of change in temperature or of wind velocity to bring about a complete wipe-out. Of course there was nowhere else to go—either land via GCA or bale out over the sea and hope to be picked up by the ageing 'Duckbutt' flying boat they used for air/sea rescue. Bluie West One offered arguably more comfortable procedures: fly overhead the airfield at a prescribed course, height and speed, descend on instruments at 300 feet a minute and graze on to the unseen icecap. Hmm! Best, they advised, to do so in formation to avoid scatter and thus be easier to find when the fog cleared. Hmm again.

I cast aside all negative prospects and brightened up at the thought that in all probability we would flit across the Atlantic in clear, cloudless conditions, unlimited visibility, light winds and with at least some of the team's VHFs working well. After all, we were 'Treble One', so we could cope easily—and, in any event, the whole venture was going to be some trip, some party.

I was startled out of my reverie by the phone bell ringing. I picked up the receiver and a voice said, 'Roger?'

'Hi Max,' I said. I had recognised the voice of Max Scannell at Operations, Fighter Command.

'It's all changed,' said Max. 'Forget North America—get yourselves out to Malta, pronto! Op Order on its way!'

'Thanks a bundle, Max,' I said.

It transpired that the Prime Minister of Malta, Dom Mintoff, had become concerned not only that Malta appeared to be about to sink under the weight of V-bombers, Canberras, maritime and sundry transport RAF aircraft arriving there in support of the Suez venture but, moreover, that the island now presented a very tempting target to the Russians, who might see the Suez operation as an opportunity to carry out an air attack. Mintoff had telephoned Prime Minister Anthony Eden and wanted to know what he was going to do about it. CAS was contacted, he contacted Fighter Command, Command found that all the day fighter squadrons had commitments that were more important than 'Treble One's jolly to North America and so now it was our turn to draw the short straw.

I made my way to the crew room and delivered my news. The pilots tittered, thinking it was my idea of a joke, but not a very good one. However, the penny soon dropped and the questions poured out. When? How many? How long for? Who's going? And so on. Our task was to get seven Hunters out to Malta as quickly as possible. Transport aircraft had been ordered for ground crews and equipment. I was to lead the detachment out and set up operations so as to provide two fully armed and operational aircraft at readiness throughout daylight hours. If the pair were scrambled, they were to be immediately replaced by two more at Standby, and so on from dawn to dusk.

And so a few days later, instead of leaving North Weald with my compass set on a westerly heading, it was firmly pointing east. With a brief refuelling stop at Istres in southern France, we soon arrived at Luqa, Malta, and were met by our own ground crew who had flown out the day before.

While our aircraft were serviced and fully armed with max ammo, we pilots familiarised ourselves with the operational procedures both of Luqa and the GCI station and met the people who would be scrambling and vector-

ing us on to any attacking aircraft. As I recall, we managed to get a pair on standby before dusk on that first day.

My orders were to return to Britain as soon as the detachment was operationally in place and exercise overall command of the Malta detachment from North Weald while at the same time try to keep the aerobatic team in being and meet any aerobatic commitments that arose. I did feel rather miffed that I could miss out if a real shooting war broke out, but the orders made sense—and, in any case, they were orders. So I quickly appointed a detachment commander and set about getting myself back to Britain.

It was at this point that I realised that the series of fast-moving events of the last few days, with seemingly endless decisions being made followed by rapid actions, were over for me, at least for the next few days. I felt quite depressed and useless. I had to bid farewell to my eager young fighter pilots when I would much rather have stayed with them, but in addition leave my Hunter in Malta and suffer the indignity of returning as a civilian passenger.

It got worse; the service from Malta to the United Kingdom was by means of a Vickers Viking. I had flown the RAF version, the Valetta, while at Farnborough and knew it to be hardly an exciting experience. And so it proved to be. As we wallowed, Wellington bomber-like, over the Mediterranean, I discovered that the agony was to be prolonged by calling in at Nice before eventually staggering into Blackbushe, seemingly endless hours after leaving Malta. And there was still an awkward rail journey ahead before arriving at North Weald.

I did make two further visits to the detachment, flying out newly serviced aircraft and bringing back those due for inspection. On such flights we always took a pair and my Number Two pilot stayed at Luqa, thus allowing a pilot exchange. Each time I made a long weekend of my visits so that I could spend time with the crews. We kept up this exchange method throughout, although on most occasions we exchanged two pilots while the ground crews were rotated as required.

As history records, the Suez venture fizzled ignominiously to an end and the detachment could return to base. During their time on operations in Malta, our aircraft never had to open fire although they were often scrambled on identification missions. The general verdict of all concerned was that the whole experience had been an enjoyable change, of both task and location.

I decided to fly out to lead our aircraft home. As we climbed out of Luqa and up over the Med, I set a westerly course and realised that such a heading was what I had looked forward to doing and then heading out over the Atlantic all those weeks ago.

I mused that Max had indeed been right: 'It's all changed.'

Below: Another view of the 'Treble One' foursome seen on page 80.

COURTESY PHILIP JARRETT

COURTESY MICHAEL THURLEY

Left: There were a number of accidents involving Hunters at North Weald, but thankfully it was only a minor 'prang' when WT720 collapsed an under-carriage leg when landing on 10 September 1956. Other North Weald Hunter accidents involved Mk 6s XF525 and XE621, which collided on 7 June 1957, and Mk 6 XF510, an aircraft used by the Station Flight, which crashed the same month after the engine failed, sadly killing the pilot.

North Weald Station Commander. Rising through the post of Air Officer Commanding No 11 Group in 1950 and Deputy Chief of the Air Staff in 1953, he became Commander-in-Chief Fighter Command in 1956 and a Marshal of the Royal Air Force—the highest rank in the Service. From this lofty position he was to give great encouragement to Topp, whose ambition was to form a first-class formation display team.

It had become the norm both before World War II and again during the late 1940s and early 1950s for the RAF's fighter squadrons to assemble their own display teams to represent them, and this tradition spawned some friendly inter-squadron competition to find a unit to represent Fighter Command itself. Initially in Meteor F.8s but at North Weald soon flying Hunter Mk 4s, No 111 had, thanks to the CO's drive and leadership, achieved a very high reputation for its prowess with its four-ship aerobatic team, and this resulted in its being selected, on merit, to work up a five-man team that would promote the RAF in air displays on the Continent and elsewhere, beginning in 1956.

Above: Marshal of the Royal Air Force Sir Thomas Pike GCB CBE DFC* DL, whose influence on North Weald was immense.

COURTESY NWAM

COURTESY NWAM

Left: Birth of the 'Black Arrows': two rare glimpses into the hangar showing, in the back-ground, No 111 Squadron's Hunters undergoing repainting in their soon-to-be-famous *décor*. The Meteor visible was the personal mount of Station CO Wing Commander Sutton.

Left: The new colours revealed: Hunter F.6 XF416 parked outside the hangar at North Weald. The five-ship No 111 Squadron formation aerobatic team was already up and running when agreement was secured to repaint the Hunters—but only five (!)—in the new all-black finish.

NO SMOKING

COURTESY NWAM

Right: Immaculate flying by No 111 Squadron as the five-man team displays its new colour scheme. Underwing serial numbers were now dispensed with, although they were carried in small red characters along the rear of the fuselage.

85

HAWKER HUNTER F. Mk 4
Type: Interceptor fighter
Engine: One 7,500lb thrust Rolls-Royce Avon 113 turbojet
Length: 45ft 10½in (13.98m)
Wing span: 33ft 8in (10.26m)
Weight: 12,550lb (5,690kg) empty
Speed: 700mph (1,130kph) max. at sea level
Service ceiling: 50,000ft (15,240m)
Armament: Four 30mm Aden cannon.
Crew: Pilot only

Below: A No 111 Squadron Hunter in 'Black Arrows' finish. The port side of the nose bore a miniature Squadron crest, the corresponding design on the starboard side being a Union flag.

Then came something truly radical, as Squadron CO Roger Topp recalls:

'I had perfected the performance of the four-aeroplane team, so it seemed reasonable to add a fifth, thus creating a new "shape" and gratifyingly going one up on the United States Air Force Skyblazer four. But why leave it there? So I gained approval from Tom Pike at Fighter Command to incorporate a fifth Hunter, then a sixth, and eventually up to nine, which in three lines of three wrote a neat "111" across the sky! At that time the Skyblazers were disporting themselves in North American F-100s carrying a lurid paint scheme of red, white and blue stars and stripes. This set me thinking about our squadron marking

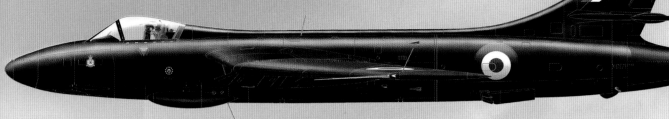

Right: A formation take-off by the five-ship team at North Weald. Precision was the watchword—from the moment the pilots entered their cockpits until final disembarkation at the close of the display.

A Question Answered

Graham Jessop

Dr Michael Thurley, a Flying Officer with the 'Black Arrows' at North Weald and now a retired GP living in Canada, writes:

'The Standard Presentation that afternoon was by Air Chief Marshal Sir Harry Broadhurst, an ex No 111 Squadron member. In the morning we had a practice with me flying Number Five, during which my pitot head became bent 90 degrees. Not wanting to report a mid-air collision with Sir Harry listening in the tower, I reported a bird strike and was instructed by Boss Topp to formate on Number Three for landing.

'My memory of the afternoon is very spotty. After the parade and presentation we did our show again and, because of strong wind, had to land downhill on Runway 05, aiming to miss the bump at the top of the hill. I didn't. This resulted in a very rough landing (I am told). My last memory is of seeing the rubber padding on the gun sight. The aircraft, with me unconscious within it, ran the length of the runway, down a drop then started knocking down lead-in light poles and breaking up. The seat fired during these impacts and delivered me away from the exploding wreck. The next thing I knew was waking up for a short period in the X-Ray Department at St. Margaret's Hospital, Epping, asking for, and getting, a cigarette. I had two fractured vertebræ, which were initially treated with a body cast that quickly became 'graffitied' with rather rude messages. I then enjoyed two months at Headley Court Rehabilitation Centre, becoming very fit with daily physiotherapy. With many thanks to the Boss, fighting the brass, I was back doing 'Form Aeros' again in July. I am very glad I did not die on that day . . .'

It's funny how time plays tricks with the memory: some things from the 1950s are very vivid while others have just disappeared. In those days the war was still on one's mind; DIY was unheard of because of the continuing shortage of building supplies for reconstruction; and food was still in limited supply (Sunday roast was only possible if father could shoot a duck or rabbit). I lived on the main road to Tilbury and I still have a very clear picture in my mind of the heavily sand-camouflaged Army vehicles passing through, ready for Suez.

Not far away was North Weald aerodrome—a hive of activity during World War II, of course, and still on 'black alert'. The sky was frequently strewn with the white streaks from the trails of aeroplanes, mainly those undertaking military exercises. My father was a schoolmaster at North Weald and he got to know some of the service families; moreover, being an ex RAF man, he still had a fascination for aircraft. Often we would go up to the airfield and watch them coming in and taking off—occasionally Spitfires but later the jets, often camouflaged ready for action if required. We were also fortunate in that the 'Black Arrows' display team was based at North Weald. What a spectacle the Hunters made as they rolled and pirouetted across the sky!

One summer we got to hear about a special air display, in which, top of the bill, would be the five Hunters of No 111 Squadron's 'Black Arrows' team. Father and I got to the perimeter fence early that day to make sure

Above: The No 111 Squadron Standard Presentation at North Weald on 30 April 1957, the prelude to an appalling accident . . .

that we had a good view, right in line with the aircraft taking off and taxying at the end of the runway. It was a memorable afternoon, and there was some stunning flying. Everyone was in fine spirits, enjoying the warm weather and good camaraderie.

Then it happened. The 'Black Arrows' had just finished their highly polished act and were returning to base and landing in formation on the airfield. Suddenly there was absolute silence. It was obvious that one of the returning aircraft was in trouble and was not going to be able to land successfully. It appeared that the pilot tried to take off again but to no avail and overshot the runway, carried on through the airfield perimeter fence, across a field, through some scrubland and eventually came to a standstill. I think the pilot tried to eject from the aircraft and managed it at the last moment. I was absolutely horrified: young lads just did not witness accidents in those days—especially not where the RAF was concerned.

Without a moment's hesitation my father said 'Come on!' and there he was, rushing across the field, with me in tow, to find out what he could do to help. He had no thought whatsoever for the potential risks of fire or explosion from the crashed aircraft, just that unfettered desire to do what he could to assist. Just as we arrived on the scene the airfield ambulance came along. The medical crew, with my father, pulled the pilot from the wreckage. I seem to recall that he was unconscious as he was placed on a stretcher and carefully transferred to the ambulance. He seemed to be in a bad way, not moving, and I remember saying to my father 'Is he alive?' By this time my father had struck up a brief conversation with the officer in charge of the recovery and he was asked for his name and address in case the RAF needed to follow anything up. It had quite a sobering effect on the day's events.

Over the years I have often wondered how the pilot fared. I thought that I would never know. On 1 May 2010, fifty-three years on and quite by chance, I got the answer!

Below: . . . when Michael Thurley's Hunter XG203/'R' suffered a very rough landing, resulting, seemingly, in a collapsed nosewheel leg . . .

Below: . . . and a horrific aftermath, all of which Graham Jessop, as a young lad, witnessed. His father helped pull the pilot clear as fire crews arrived at the scene.

HAWKER HUNTER F. Mk 6
Type: Interceptor and ground-attack fighter
Engine: One 10,000lb thrust Rolls-Royce Avon 203 turbojet
Length: 45ft 10½in (13.98m)
Wing span: 33ft 8in (10.26m)
Weight: 12,760lb (5,785kg) empty
Speed: 710mph (1,145kph) max. at sea level
Service ceiling: 50,000ft (15,240m)
Armament: Four 30mm Aden cannon plus underwing stores.
Crew: Pilot only

Right: 'The Five' in tight form-ation as they practise their magic. Later, a modification to the paint scheme saw the wing and fuselage roundels, and the fin flashes, outlined in white.

Above: A memento of the 'Black Arrows'—a publicity photo-graph complete with portraits and facsimile signatures of (left to right) Squadron Leader Topp (Leader and Squadron CO), Flight Lieutenants Paddy Hine and Les Swart, and Flying Officers Bob Barcilon and Michael Thurley.
Right: Four further photographs illustrating the superb aerobatic skills of the five founder members of the 'Black Arrows'.

COURTESY MICHAEL THURLEY

COURTESY PHILIP JARRETT

Abov: Two photographs illustrating vehicles used by the vital support personnel at North Weald during the 1950s.

of a black bar either side of the fuselage roundel, which dated back to well before the war. It struck me that an all-black Hunter would look pretty damned good, and I got Tom Pike's permission to try it on just one aeroplane. After he had seen the finished article I persuaded him to allow us to paint the core team of five all black, but no more; after all, the RAF had spent years devising carefully designed patterns of camouflage and deciding where roundels should be placed, the style for code numbers, and what squadron insignia might be displayed. All this was more or less immutable, and approval for anything else would be refused. However, I began noticing that a Hunter would be in a hangar for routine servicing one afternoon and would emerge, perhaps a couple of days later, gloss black overall. Happily, everyone followed my example of looking the other way, and there was general agreement that the aircraft looked magnificent. Even the public relations people in the Air Ministry had to admit that the enthusiastic response of the public to performances by the "Black Arrows" was all they could possibly hope for. We had the French press to thank for the team's name: we had given a number of earlier displays in France before the black scheme was adopted, but one reporter wrote that against a sunlit blue sky the team resembled *"flèches noires".'*

The year 1957 saw the birth of a nine-ship team but the Squadron was about to say farewell to North Weald. On 19 February 1958, The 'Treble One' Hunters took off from the old aerodrome for the very last time,

Right: It was a sad day when, on 19 February 1958, 'Treble-One' bade farewell to North Weald: no more would a front-line RAF squadron be based there. The impact on the neighbourhood was keenly felt, too, as local businesses experienced the downturn in fortunes. Even the local branch railway seemed to sympathise, as the old steam trains were replaced by 'tube' type London Transport stock and the North Weald goods yard closed.

Above: The last Squadron CO—Squadron Leader (as he then was) Roger Topp AFC*.

Right: The abrupt disbandment of the Auxiliary squadrons in 1957 was marked at airfields the length and breadth of the country, with mock 'funerals' and 'burials' commonplace. This pithy epitaph was the work of personnel of No 601 Squadron at North Weald.

bound, via North Luffenham, for Wattisham, to begin a long association with the Suffolk airfield. The 'Black Arrows' went on, under Roger Topp, to greater glory, forming a sixteen-Hunter aerobatic team and, ultimately, a 22-aircraft formation which included in its repertoire an immaculate mass loop—to this day the largest formation of aeroplanes ever to have undertaken the manœuvre as a single entity.

For the last twelve months of their tenure, No 111 had been the sole RAF squadron operating from North Weald, as in 1957 major political decisions had brought about seismic changes within the Service. This was the year of the British Government's now notorious Defence White Paper, which opined that manned fighters were things of the past and that, in future, the RAF, and hence the Defence of the Realm, would be structured around unmanned guided missiles. As part of the programme of defence cuts, it had been decided to disband the Royal Auxiliary Air Force in its entirety and, as a result, Nos 601 and 604 Squadrons peremptorily disappeared into oblivion, both units disbanding on 10 March 1957.

With the final departure of Treble One, the prospects for North Weald as an operational airfield looked very bleak . . .

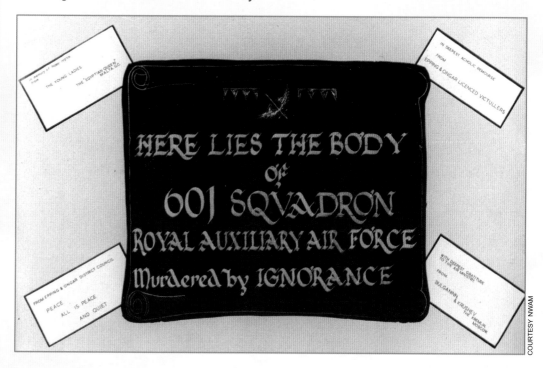

HERE LIES THE BODY OF 601 SQVADRON ROYAL AUXILIARY AIR FORCE Murdered by IGNORANCE

PRESENT AND FUTURE

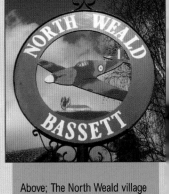

IN the late 1950s, the designation of new airlanes out of Heathrow placed severe restrictions on military activity in the skies over west Essex and, in any case, North Weald's runways were too short for the English Electric Lightning, the RAF's new supersonic fighter. Hence the RAF no longer had a requirement for front-line flying from the airfield. For a brief period after No 111 Squadron departed, from February to May 1958, the Battle of Britain Flight was stationed at North Weald, with one Hurricane and five Spitfires on its inventory. Over the years that followed, several small units, including the Aircrew Selection Branch, used North Weald airfield as their base, but by September 1964 the site had been reduced to 'Inactive' and the RAF relinquished it to Army use. The York and Lancaster Regiment were stationed here until 1968, earning the Freedom of Epping during their tenure. The West Essex and East Hert-fordshire Gliding Club took advantage of the site, and the Air Training Corps used the buildings and flew gliders. The old married quarters were sold to a housing trust and, although renovated, these buildings can still

Above; The North Weald village sign, located not far from the entrance to the airfield and unveiled by Sir Thomas Pike, commemorates the wartime rôle played by servicemen and women and by villagers alike.

Left: As it was: the main entrance to RAF North Weald, photographed in the mid-1950s when the airfield was still an active Fighter Command station. Little visible here remains today, although the Station Office at far left is still *in situ*—see page 95.
Below: During the 1970s the RAF buildings gradually fell into disrepair. Seen here during that time are the main A type hangars, the MT (Motor Transport) accommodation and the Station Chapel.

COURTESY NWAM

COURTESY NWAM

COURTESY NWAM

Right: A photograph taken during the production of the film *The Battle of Britain*, which was released to cinemas in London in 1969—appropriately, on Battle of Britain Day, 15 September.

Below: One unfortunate occurrence at North Weald took place on 11 June 1962 when the world's only airworthy Bristol Bulldog, K2227, suffered a landing accident. The aircraft was repaired, but later crashed again. It now resides in the RAF Museum at Hendon.

Right: North Weald was for many years during the 1970s and 1980s the host airfield for major international air shows, first the International Air Tattoo (1971–72), then the occasional Royal Air Force Association display (1973–82) and later the Fighter Meet (until 1997). Various activities of this nature still take place at North Weald. Here a beautifully preserved P-39 Airacobra, in Russian markings, has caught the photographer's eye at one of the annual events.

be recognised today as of the pattern of all wartime airfield accommodation. The housing was finally purchased by Epping Forest District Council. In general, however, the 1960s was a decade of peace and quiet for the local residents, and the buildings and facilities on the airfield gradually fell into disrepair.

An uncanny rebirth was to come about in 1968, when North Weald was selected as one of the locations for the production of the United Artists film *The Battle of Britain* (Duxford, another famous RAF wartime station not far to the north, was also employed in this way). Many scenes in the film can be recognised as having been shot at North Weald, and for a whole summer, the roar of Rolls-Royce Merlin engines was to be heard again as September 1940 was re-fought in the skies overhead.

The world-renowned Royal International Air Tattoo, currently held annually at RAF Fairford in Gloucestershire, had its beginnings in 1971 at North Weald. Then called the Air Tattoo, it was a one-day event, and its proximity to London virtually guaranteed huge attendances. Foreign

participation from the European air forces increased from year to year, and the event offered an ideal opportunity for old friends, for example the Norwegian Air Force, to return to their wartime base. A victim of its own success, the Tattoo outgrew the acreage at North Weald and eventually it was obliged to find a new home at RAF Greenham Common.

The popularity of air shows at North Weald did not fade, however, as the annual Fighter Meet was staged here after originating at West Malling. For some fourteen years the Meet, quickly growing into a two-day event, was held, much to the delight of increasing crowds, until an encroaching motorway, difficulties concerning the regular open-air market (held every other weekend on the airfield—and very successful) and new flightpaths over west Essex brought about its demise—but not before rock music and air shows combined to bring to the public a extra dimension to flying displays. Dave Gilmour, guitarist with the well-known band Pink Floyd, had over the years built up a collection of aircraft (all airworthy) known as the Intrepid Aviation Company. These machines, housed at North Weald, came to form the centrepiece of some excellent air shows, with military participation and huge attendances.

Increasingly since the end of World War II, both businessmen and the military have steadily collected together, rebuilt (where necessary) and

Top: North Weald is nowadays home to a number of vintage aircraft, including the Hangar 11 collection, owned by Peter Teichman. The collection includes the rare Hurricane Mk IIB and the P-51D Mustang seen here.

COURTESY NWAM

AUTHOR

Above right: All manner of aircraft are seen at North Weald today. This two-seat Vampire T.11, for example, owned by the Vampire Preservation Group, is based here and is often to be seen in the skies around the airfield.

Left: Although it has now been joined by two others flying in the United States, Supermarine Seafire SX336 was for some years the only airworthy representative of the type in the world. It was restored, and is currently operated, by Kennet Aviation at North Weald; it is seen here during a display at Duxford. A two-seat Sea Fury for the Royal Navy Historic Flight, VX281, has recently (September 2010) been restored to flying condition by the same company.

flown (if feasible) veteran aircraft sourced from all over the world. In the main, these have tended to be aircraft famous for their part during the war, but many of an earlier vintage, as well as jets from the 1950s and 1960s, have been lovingly restored both for static and flying use.

Those aeroplanes in regular demand for both film and display work use tend to be based at a selected few airfields in Great Britain, and North Weald has for some years been one of the principal sites in use for this purpose. Companies such as Aces High were early participants in the aircraft preservation business, regularly making available both aircraft and pilots for work within the film and television industries. Programmes such as *Band of Brothers* and *Charlotte Grey* are but two that have benefited from this service.

The restoration and preservation of elderly aircraft involves incredible dedication. It requires thousands of hours to rebuild an aircraft whose original manufacturers stopped keeping spares some fifty or more years ago, it is a costly pursuit, and it is subject to present-day safety rules, not those of the 1940s. The ambition is always to produce, or reproduce, an immaculate aircraft faithful in every way possible to its original. Many people would consider that their value, both financial and historic, means that these aircraft should never be risked by actually flying them, but thankfully there are those who believe that such aircraft should fly—if possible.

One of these people is Peter Teichman, who owns the Hangar 11 collection at North Weald. Including as it does a Hurricane (a rare Mk II), a Spitfire (the only flying Mk XI in the world), a P-51D Mustang and a P-40

ROGER COOK

Left: North Weald's links with the Norwegian Air Force, forged more than 65 years ago when Nos 331 and 332 Squadrons flew from the airfield, remain robust, even in the twenty-first century. Here a Norwegian F-16 brakes as it lands for a courtesy visit.

AUTHOR

Left: Links with the many squadrons that have served with North Weald over the years also remain strong. Here a Shorts Tucano of No 72 Squadron calls in for the RAFA Battle of Britain Sunset Social Evening in August 2010.

Kittyhawk, these valuable vintage aircraft are individually amongst the very best of all 'warbirds' whether judged from the point of view of looks, of originality or of the manner in which they are flown. Often to be seen practising in the skies of northern Essex, Peter has gained a huge reputation and considers himself a 'custodian of history', and has therefore, with the other 'warbird' operators, helped to keep alive a flying memorial to those that flew from this green field before them.

Visitors today to North Weald can be forgiven if they are almost overcome by a sense of turning back the clock, for history is a major part of the airfield. There are, however, those here who in the twenty-first century

Below: Treats for the aviation enthusiast are frequent. In the summer of 2010, aircraft from the Battle of Britain Memorial Flight, during a salute of wartime Fighter Command airfields, made an overnight visit. Peter Vacher's Hurricane R4118—a genuine Battle of Britain aircraft—joined them, and is seen here departing, with St Andrew's Church visible in the background.

Above: Retired aircrew with an association with North Weald also drop by from time to time: (top left) fighter ace Air Vice-Marshal Johnnie Johnson signs the Museum's Visitors' Book in 1986, and (right) Airfield Historian Arthur Moreton with Battle of Britain veterans.

Above: The vitality of the airfield is maintained today, thanks to the support of many first-class businesses located at various points around the perimeter.

are inspiring the fliers of tomorrow. A further glance around the western dispersal reveals not only fascinating veteran but also truly modern, carbon-fibre aircraft. Having devoured the spectacular panorama, one can grab a mug of tea (or something stronger) at The Squadron, one of the many important businesses based here and one with a social centre and refreshment room housed within an old Nissen hut that serves to remind the patron of stirring days now gone.

If time allows, though, it is worth venturing back to the opposite side of the airfield, to Ad Astra House, where the North Weald Airfield Museum is based. To the front of the building are both a poignant memorial to those who served here (incorporating a Debt of Honour to all who gave their lives), and the commemorative obelisk presented many years ago by Princess Astrid of Norway. The inside of this building allows one to retrace all that history recorded at this famous aerodrome, and to remember that the skies of Essex were not always peaceful but will for ever hold their place in our history.

Per Ardua ad Astra.

Above: Ad Astra House, the former Station Office at the main entrance to the airfield, in 1980. The Museum is now accommodated here.
Right: Ad Astra House as it is today, with the wartime memorials that now front it.

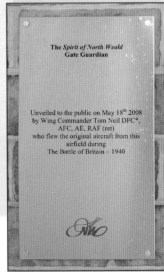

The *Spirit of North Weald*
Gate Guardian

Unveiled to the public on May 18th 2008
by Wing Commander Tom Neil DFC*,
AFC, AE, RAF (ret)
who flew the original aircraft from this
airfield during
The Battle of Britain – 1940

Left: The Memorial Window in
Ad Astra House, home of the
North Weald Airfield Museum.
Above: The plaque marking the
unveiling of the gate guardian.

Above: St Andrew's Church, off
the north-eastern edge of the
airfield.
Below: St Andrew's churchyard
—the last resting place of some
of North Weald's fallen heroes.

Below: Looking north from the
airfield today—a view little
changed since 1916. Weald
Hall, part of which is visible at
far left, has seen it all.

AUTHOR